The CRISIS In

AFRO-AMERICAN LEADERSHIP

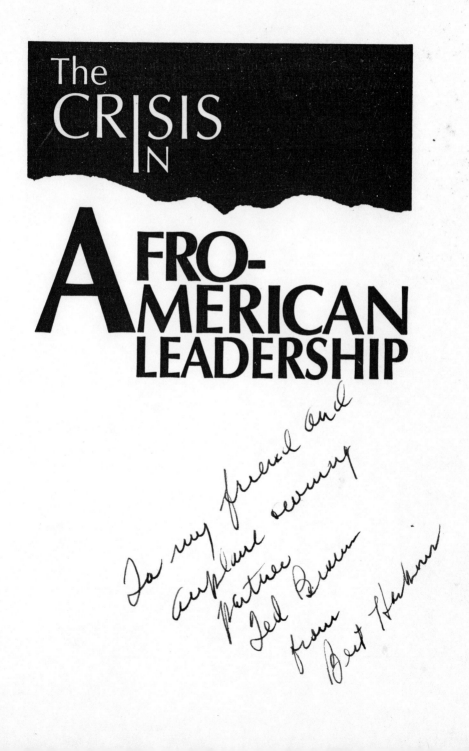

To my friend and airplane servicing partner Ted Brown from Burt Hackman

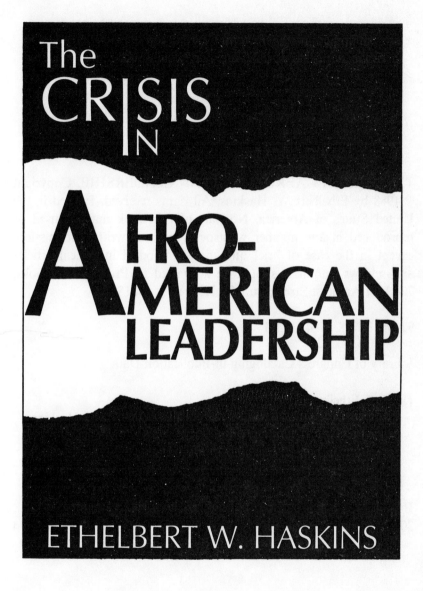

The CRISIS In AFRO-AMERICAN LEADERSHIP

ETHELBERT W. HASKINS

PROMETHEUS BOOKS
700 East Amherst Street, Buffalo, New York 14215

91 90 89 88   4 3 2 1

Library of Congress Cataloging-in-Publication Data

Haskins, Ethelbert W., 1921-
    The crisis in Afro-American leadership/Ethelbert W. Haskins.
        p.   cm.
    Bibliography: p.
    ISBN 0-87975-450-8 : $19.95
    1. Afro-American leadership. I. Title.
E 185.615.H327   1988
303.3'4'08996073—dc19   88-4134
                                                        CIP

CONTENTS

III. The Golden Century of Afro-American Leadership

Great Leaders of the Past

The Negro Press

IV. Afro-American Leadership and Education

V. Afro-American Leadership: Religion and Social Morality

VI. Afro-American Leadership and Faith

ACKNOWLEDGMENTS

I am indebted to Lloyd and Mary Morain for their encouragement and painstaking reading of the manuscript and their many suggestions which I gratefully incorporated into the work. I would like to express my appreciation to Karen Hart, Alice Stein, and Jannelle Walden-Agyeman for their careful editoral readings and comments. And I would like to thank Edd Doerr for his suggestions, Susan Torcaso for typing the final draft, and Bill Toler for bringing relevant magazine and newspaper articles to my attention over the years.

Chapter 1
THE DILEMMA

1. A Loser Psychology

Every quarter-century has its quirks. Historic, economic, and socio-logical forces since the early 1960s have conspired to midwife a unique new mentality in the United States.

Afro-American youth in the decaying center-city ghettos represent the largest group in the history of the country to consider itself disadvantaged and at the same time remain uncommitted to self-betterment. These young people are poverty ridden and for the most part functionally illiterate. If this double-barreled infirmity is not sufficient to keep them out of the American mainstream, they are beset with a more disastrous malady. They lack enough faith in them-selves to help themselves.

Illiteracy and poverty are not necessarily terminal. Such afflicted groups have arrived in America since its inception. But without exception, they steer by the star of self-betterment. As a first priority they set out in pursuit of literacy—learning to speak, read, and write mainstream English and acquiring the ability to understand and be understood in the marketplace, in the employment emporium, and in social intercourse.

The linguistic aspirations manifested by the self-betterment men-tality are in stark contrast with the prevailing attitude in the black ghetto where the linkage between self-improvement and the improve-ment of one's position often goes undiscerned. A perverse romanticism is maintained in defense of "black English." Not only are grammar, cadence, emphasis, and inflections formulated in deliberate deviation from mainstream communication patterns, but new expressions are whimsically invented and discarded. A few months' absence from the "scene" renders one practically incapable of following a substantial part of an ongoing conversation.

A "dangerous drift" that impedes understanding between the black ghetto and mainstream America is well under way, according to an April 1985 *Washington Post* article entitled "Black-White Schism in Speech Seen Widening." It quotes linguistic research reports from the University of Pennsylvania and the University of Illinois (Chicago) maintaining that, among other disadvantages, the language disparity locks ghetto dwellers out of important networks that could lead to "employment, housing, and basic rights and privileges."

2. Racism Ideology and the New Enslavement

The presence of despair, rather than hope, in the human breast is an acquired rather than a natural phenomenon. The quality that made *Homo sapiens* human was the will to make step-by-step improvements based on experience. This included increasingly harmonious relationships within society and a more constructive functional understanding of the physical environment.

A seminal cause of the ghetto brand of hopelessness has apparently gone unnoticed by the social engineers and pundits within whose province these observations are customarily relegated. General befuddlement is revealed in the numerous myopic reports and opinions commonly conceding that opportunities in the center cities have been eroding over the last decade. Of those concerned with the problem, the various black studies departments associated with many of the nation's colleges and universities have carved out for themselves special intellectual and psychological hegemony. Over the years since the discipline was crafted with a great deal of sound and fury in the 1960s, black studies has arrived at what its proponents would like to have the community believe is a social science. It has a literature, a definition of terms, and a methodology for prioritizing and interpreting facts and occurrences.

From the very beginning black studies was contoured to launch mainstream America, including the Afro-American middle class, on a sustained guilt trip. It dedicated its energies to exposing the bare fangs of racism and the bruised and battered figures it left strewn over the landscape. Living on the business end of racism became the "black experience" and its results, the "black condition." And the lexicon had an addendum. Any unconvinced Afro-American was either too insensitive to realize his straits or without sympathy for his more unfortunate "brothers," or, even more pathetic, a racist masochist.

Social sciences are celebrated for their intramural dissent. So respected a field of inquiry as economics, with its saints and savants and econometric models, is notorious for the spectacle of equally eminent scholars perched on opposite ends of analytic and prognostic seesaws. But from the outset, the architects of black studies constructed anti-dissent firebreaks into their discipline. Differences of opinion on any fundamental point were met with emotional charges of racism—by design or by ignorance of the black experience. Having put the cart before the horse, they developed a viewpoint which suffers from the lack of the kind of balanced discussion that makes for introspection. All too often black studies has unnecessarily settled into a single-issue posture. According to its gospel, racism is the sole source of everything askew in the black ghetto. Conversation became catechismal rather than give-and-take. And what gave promise of becoming a social science has almost degenerated into an ideology.

Some spokesmen for the inner-city ghetto take their cues and derive their credentials from the black studies ideology. Too many of the thoughts they articulate concerning the black condition are confined to an exposition of the anatomy and evils of racism and the impotence of its victims.

Whatever observers outside of the center city think of this assessment of racism and impotence they keep to themselves. When the subject arises it is politely circumvented or addressed with circumspection. It is easy to be intimidated by the ideologue's ire. How does one answer a public accusation of evil and ignorance? But in the black ghetto there is no such quandary. The ideology of racism commands a solid phalanx of true believers. And their conviction of helplessness and hopelessness leaves them in psychological bondage: a new enslavement is their legacy fostered by the single-issue racism ideology.

3. The Heroic Atrocity

Unfortunately, the black studies mentality seldom focuses beyond studying, researching, codifying, exposing, and condemning racism—defining its evils and understanding its victims—to a degree that ensures psychic surrender. This mentality—unlike that of the thousands of Afro-Americans whose performance in business, in the professions, and in the ordinary walks of life categorize them in the mainstream—insists that the ghetto dwellers are helpless and hopeless. For too long it has permitted one looming consideration to eclipse the scores of other problems that weigh on the shoulders of the clients it is committed to serve. It has distorted its holy obligation into what Bertrand Russell might have called a heroic atrocity. Diagnosis is not an end in itself. Its purpose is to make possible a prescription with reasonable prospects for effecting a cure. And "reasonable prospects" assumes significance when relief in the ghetto is so often portrayed as being dependent upon a reordered "system." Imagine the bleak outlook of a youngster whose solitary recourse is to await an about-face of the only system he has ever known, and to suspect, hopelessly, that this will not happen in his lifetime.

The problems of the black ghetto are too varied and complex for a single-issue ideology. Functional illiteracy, for example, has nothing to do with racism. The schools are there in large numbers. Books are available and qualified teachers are on the scene. The lacking ingredients are discipline and motivation, imposed at an early enough age to direct the students on their cerebral quest. A child who learns to read early usually falls into the habit of additional reading to satisfy a natural curiosity. By the same token, an early no-nonsense intro-duction to arithmetic generates a desire to investigate qualities and quantities. And enough literary and arithmetic curiosity generated in a reasonably nurturing environment helps propel one into the main-stream of thought and ideas.

Mainstream America is not exclusively "white," as many in the black ghetto believe. There are millions of whites who do *not* belong. Mainstream America is a state of mind, and participation is open to anyone. It is a can-do condition of preparation, ambition, communi-cation, accomplishment, and awareness. Entrants are welcome, and they are expected to comprehend, contribute to, and appreciate the activities, accomplishments, and prevailing nuances. The mainstream is also an accumulation of opportunities, benefits, and gratifications. It is a conviction that problems can be coped with and tomorrows can be fashioned as improvements upon today.

The thrust of the ideologues should be redirected toward the manufacture of messages of how-to and optimism and inspiration. Encouragement inspires. Individuals turn naturally toward prospects of improvement.

Except for the Negro youth in the center-city ghetto, every group in the world considers the United States to be synonymous with opportunity. The universities, colleges, and technical schools are inundated with applications from hopeful young Americans of every race who aspire with justified confidence to a brighter future. And people around the world, from Saigon to Surinam to Somalia, take chances with their lives—some virtually setting out to sea in sieves— to seek their fortunes here. It is one of the ironies of the times that the black youngster in the ghetto is encouraged by those who claim to have his interests at heart to spurn the opportunities the "system" offers and to scratch at his roots and maintain his identity until the system retools to conform to his lifestyle. Having been advised that he is life's victim and to feel sorry for himself, he sits seething in rage about his poverty and unemployment. Yet in the classified advertising section of the newspaper in which he is perusing the comics, employers are calling for electronic technicians, computer programmers, television and radio repairmen, automobile mechanics, typists, carpenters, and hundreds of other skills. It is possible that no one to whom the youngster is tuned in has ever told him the most elementary facts of employment. Throughout the history of civilization, employable people have been those prepared to perform the tasks that the community in which they live is willing to pay to have done. The tasks evolve out of community needs and dynamics. They are not tailored to fit personalities but quite the other way around.

Single-track racism ideology has had negative results. True, racism must be confronted whenever it obstructs civil rights or liberties. And there is a jurisprudence available to grapple with this recurring pestilence. But the ideology of racism has no place as an obsession, and certainly none as an obstruction.

Recently, an attempt to analyze the cultural imperatives of various groups who are failing to cope is coming into vogue. A case in point is an article, "The Origins of the Underclass," which appeared in the June and July 1986 issues of *The Atlantic*. The author, Nicholas Lemann, correctly ascribes the critical problems of the black ghetto to the black underclass culture. His assessment represents a step in the right direction. It represents a departure from the tired contention, abroad since the 1960s, which insists upon laying the blame of the plight of the center city on the "system." But a single step in the right direction is not enough.

A people's culture consists of its ideas and beliefs; its way of conducting its affairs. And the cultural parameters are set by the people's religion and their leadership. So in the final analysis the problems with a culture are problems with its leadership, the signals the leadership transmits and the ideas it espouses.

4. Education for Failure

Thousands of students pass through twelve years of ghetto schooling without ever learning the rudiments of study. These unfortunate eighteen-year-olds represent the graduates, not the dropouts in whom one might expect the disability. This fact may seem incredible to the remainder of society where high school graduation customarily requires mastery of the preparation of lessons, themes, and term papers. And this disability accounts for many of the community's employment and social problems, not the least of which is the bitter resentment the graduate feels for being treated "unfairly" when he presents himself for a job and is unable to fill out the required forms. If the unprepared pupils were held back occasionally, the process could be used as leverage to encourage all students to study. Special help should be provided where necessary.

Under present conditions, it is not long before students realize that promotion in school is automatic, without any need of exertion. They discover very early that a special dispensation exists to protect them from the rigors of thinking, and from that point, they expect to receive the rewards of work without working. Their entire encounter with school is a distortion of reality and a clear indication that their society has low expectations for them.

Occasionally, though not often enough, a few of the ghetto graduates have culturally extraneous visions of self-betterment and present themselves for education at one of their municipal junior colleges. They can be spotted right away in freshman mathematics because they rarely have their homework and always do poorly on the first test.

These students have never been clearly shown that passing a test can be reasonably accomplished by concentrating closely in class, attempting the homework every night, asking questions in the next class period about problems they were unable to solve, keeping a clear and understandable notebook, and studying the notes before the next test. Once they are clearly instructed on the techniques for surviving in an intellectual environment and held accountable under the threat of failing, more than half will show increasing improvement on successive tests. The others are unwilling or unable to change. A few respond with frustrated hostility at being instructed to revise old habits and do the "impossible." They persist, among other things, in continuing their use of "ax" (ask) and "mines" (mine), and in wearing their baseball caps in the classroom. But the culturally obstinate also serve. Their failing grades can be used as graphic examples of the fate of the perverse for those who follow in their footsteps.

Shelter against the rigors of learning is not sought for the offspring of the middle and upper economic classes in this country. On the contrary, children of parents who have high expectations for them are often sent to more strict and demanding schools. These young people learn the habits and techniques relevant to the mainstream. They are required to survive under regimens of discipline and study which the average ghetto youngster does not comprehend. And after twelve years these more privileged students are ready to move smoothly into college and thence to one of the higher rungs of the world's competitive ladders, with the salaries, opportunities, and self-esteem that the ladders' upper rungs offer.

5. A Need to Change Directions

If the considerable energy and ingenuity devoted to maintaining dog-
matic racism could be employed to establish and promulgate hope
and self-esteem, the principal problems of the black ghetto would
diminish significantly and perhaps in time disappear.

The conversion will not be easy for the ideologues. Locked in
as they are to analysis and negativism, abandoning their comfortable
viewpoints will be difficult. To turn from doomsaying to encouragement, and from waving the dour flag of despair before the people
whose interest they champion, to treating the ghetto dwellers as self-
respecting citizens who are able and willing to join the self-improvement
community is truly "an idea whose time has come." The ideologues
would begin to see the results they say they have wanted for the
last twenty years.

6. The Ideologues' Rejoinder

Over the years the black studies establishment has squandered far
too much muscle on the defense of its province. While its thesis had
some validity when it originated in the mid-1960s, it appears now
to have become a magnificent obsession entangled in a time warp.

In reply to a survey that solicited opinions concerning an article
excerpted from Chapter 2 that appeared in the July/August 1985
issue of the *Humanist,* the heads of the black studies departments
of some of the country's leading universities registered their rejoinders.
They were uniformly incensed at the suggestions that today's Afro-
American leadership is remiss in its duties to the ghetto youth, that
center city youth should be told how to break the cycle of poverty
and illiteracy, and that they are not stranded or beyond self-help.

The replies included a fusillade of the incendiary clichés that have
intimidated dissenters for more than two decades. The retorts were
laced with accusations of "false assumptions" and an "insensitive
inability" to understand the effect of the "stymied aspirations," the
"savage consequences of racism," and the "failed democratic institutions" on the young people "living without hope" in an "inescapable
ghetto."

The ideologues certainly merit credit for the clever and articulate attack they launch on ideas discordant to the assumptions that validate their professions. But they merit *discredit,* however, for the climate of despair they keep alive in the center city. Imagine the cyclone of frustration created by the authoritative voice of lamentation chanted in the ears of an entire generation! And, unfortunately, the mainstream news media reinforce the ideologues' contention. Whenever the black ghetto is examined in print or electronically, the focus is on poverty, crime, illiteracy, early illegitimate parenthood, or all four. The stories make for interesting reporting but are definite disincentives for self-improvement.

Frozen as they are in a mental state appropriate for the era preceding the enactment of the civil rights laws of the 1960s, the ideologues' opinions are patently counterproductive. Their pronouncements blatantly dishearten the youth from work, study, developing self-pride, or for bettering themselves in any discernible way. Instead, the young people smoulder in a permanent anti-social, self-loathing, self-destructive, decivilizing world hatred.

This attitude is reflected in dozens of ways. For example, the males habitually sit on the steps and in the doorways of their apartment buildings, scowling menacingly at anyone who has the affrontery to attempt to squeeze past. They amble defiantly in the crosswalks of their neighborhood streets, irascibly challenging the traffic, sometimes bringing it to a screeching halt. In fact, after their cacophonous music, obstructing the doorways and sauntering in the crosswalks have for years characterized the special petty brand of black ghetto spite. And, all too often, the black youth receive their greatest satisfaction from membership in gangs—where the blind lead the blind.

7. The Need for a Winner's Blueprint

Young inhabitants of the center cities would have been far better served had the racism ideologues pursued careers in fields other than black studies. The youth deserve a reprieve from the liturgy of doom emanating from their "expert" advocates.

If their closed minds were ventilated by the fresh air of reality, the ideologues could turn their professionalism to good account. The considerable energy spent researching and explaining the black youth's impossible estate could be redirected 180 degrees and expended on why self-help and self-actualization are necessary, and on the hows of implementing them. There are dozens of avenues onto which such upbeat efforts could be directed.

The loser's literature of the last two decades could be revised to accentuate the positive. If a non-English-speaking arrival can alight here and become a respectable middle-class wage-earner within a few years, it is profane to believe that an intelligent native cannot do as much. Doing so is no more than a matter of incentive and encouragement. The literature could include pamphlets and brochures complete with eye-catching diagrams and sketches to distribute in the schools. The schools could receive a sustained flood of such messages until they assume a community resonance and become a part of its ethos.

Education could be depicted as a golden opportunity rather than the effort in futility or the avoidable scourge that the ghetto youth customarily consider it—as a civilizing imperative, a necessary precursor for understanding the complex forces attending a high-tech society, and the surest way out of the ghetto squalor and its entrapping mentality. Education is the only insurance against falling back into the clutches of the ghetto once the exit is accomplished. In many cases young people who use athletic ability as an escape mechanism tumble backward with a thud when they fail in the major leagues before jettisoning the ghetto mentality.

Each hour in school could be depicted as a period to be put to good use and, if wasted, never to be recaptured. The quality of one's future in an increasingly complex world depends upon how well the roughly 12,000 school hours are utilized.

Specific educational programs concerning the disastrous disadvantages of early parenthood could be introduced into the community at the elementary school level. Adolescent pregnancy and parenthood could be shown as the crippling liabilities they are rather than the mark of accomplishment and the bond for cementing relationships, as the immature ghetto mentality believes.

The arrival of an infant to teenaged parents portends a speed-up in their physical world and a deceleration of their cultural and psychological worlds. It narrows the female's focus to a struggle for the survival of another helpless and demanding individual in addition to herself, and it materially strengthens her cocoon of disadvantage. Having yet to attain the maturity and experience necessary to make rational and long-range plans and assessments, the primitive urgency to survive prevents her from acquiring the perspicacity needed to better her plight or even cope with the ordinary vicissitudes of life. And she is forever deprived of the daydreams and wonderment and romanticisms that align one on the track to maturity and realism.

The combined physical acceleration and intellectual slowdown impose a Daliesque distortion on the teenaged mother's perspective. And with reality out of focus, her prospects of escaping her virtual *mondo cane* or enjoying any of life's middle-class amenities diminish from remote to naught.

An acute need exists for brochures concerning social conduct. They could explain the benefits of courtesy and good manners and the drawbacks of boorishness. Dozens of examples could be designed to illustrate how friendliness generates a positive atmosphere where productive social intercourse is possible, and how hostility creates a negative and, at times, lethal atmosphere.

What with the ghetto penchant for junk food, special instruction and brochures on nutrition would also be useful. These tracts could introduce children to the vitamin alphabet and teach them about the harm of excessive fats and salts. The knowledge would be especially useful in a community where obesity and cholesterol-induced arteriosclerosis are abiding afflictions.

Brochures could outline the dangers of smoking. Their diagrams could delineate the long-range injury to the brain when the hemoglobins are regularly shortchanged of oxygen, and the price that is exacted on the heart, lungs, DNA architecture, and brain under the attack of tars and nicotine from tobacco, and tetrahydrocannabinol from marijuana. They could illustrate what befalls the human physiology when alcohol is ingested and decomposes into its component substances and when quantities of carbon monoxide enter the bloodstream. In addition to the hygienic know-how they would disseminate, the brochures might spark the imagination of a potential chemist, physiologist, or medical technician.

Television messages and, especially, radio spots on stations where the youth have their "Walkmen" tuned in could be devised to supplement and reinforce the pamphlets.

It is no longer enough to continue diagnosing the disabilities of the ghetto youth and pointing the finger of accusation at the "system" that supposedly inflicted the injuries. The present time and common judgment require prescriptions for the malady. Because whenever an ethnic group stays in sore straits too much longer than the normal assimilation period required for its country, region, or community, it clearly and indisputably has a leadership problem.

The advocacy of a defeatist psychology is principally confined to those who assume the modern leadership roles, and, of course, to the unfortunates who give credence to the leaders' gloomy philosophy. These often gratuitous prolocutors presume to speak to and for the Afro-Americans who have not gotten into resonance with mainstream rhythms. And apparently the prognosticators fail to discern that their negativism serves to exacerbate the problems of their constituency. This fact is borne out by the spectacular results of the high-expectation projects in education operated by Marva Collins in Chicago and John Nettles in Anniston, Alabama. (Both will be referred to in detail later.)

The significant accomplishments in the Afro-American community are made by the individuals and groups who give short shrift to the defeatists' pronouncements, who believe just the opposite of what the negativists preach. The thirty-nine Afro-American-owned banks with assets exceeding 1.5 billion dollars, and the Afro-American-owned businesses whose sales amounted to more than 3 billion dollars in 1986 and who made *Black Enterprise*'s Top One Hundred List are hardly operated by people who acquiesce to the "hopeless" theory. Moreover, the 1,104,150 Afro-American students between the ages of fourteen and thirty-four, 80 percent of whom were attending mainstream rather than minority colleges in 1983 according to the *Digest of Education Statistics* (1987), hardly subscribed to the anachronistic law that aspirations for self-betterment are futile. Furthermore, according to the same source, minority enrollment in colleges increased by more than 85 percent during the decade of 1973-1983, while the population increase was less than 18 percent. Every significant pointer indicates that the leadership concentration on negativism is out of sync with the reality of the times.

Chapter 2
THE PRESENT PREDICAMENT IN AFRO-AMERICAN LEADERSHIP

1. Prominent Leaders of the Past

One of the earmarks of the 1970s was the absence of Afro-American leadership in the United States. This malady is wearing on into the 1980s, and unless either the psycho-technical climate, or those aspiring to leadship, undergo a radical change, nothing on the landscape presages effective leadership in the foreseeable future. In fact, the image of Afro-American leadership has fallen into such questionable repute, for obvious as well as subtle and complex reasons, that only the incompetent or the crass opportunist will make more than a self-conscious feint at the role. This absence of Negro leadership, having prevailed for two decades, is unique to the last 160 years. From early in the nineteenth century into the second decade of the latter half of the twentieth, an unbroken succession of dynamic, enlightened, and concerned men stood at the helm of the Afro-American community's aspirations.

John Russwurm was the first Negro to graduate from an American institution of higher learning. In the 1820s he left Bowdoin College and arrived in New York City to found the first Negro newspaper, *Freedom's Journal.* From that venture onward, until the death of Martin Luther King, Jr., in the 1960s, the Afro-American community had a unifying focal point.

While *Freedom's Journal* was still at the apex of its influence, Frederick Douglass came on the scene as the featured speaker of the Massachusetts Anti-Slavery Society. His entrance into the abolition and

Negro rights struggle was followed in rapid sequence by Booker T. Washington and W. E. Du Bois. During the first half of the 1890s the lives and participation of this trio overlapped in the leadership firmament. But the overlapping years represented the last of Douglass's life. He died in 1895 at the age of seventy-eight. Washington, who was nearly forty years younger, died of exhaustion only twenty years later.

Symmetrically timed at the halfway point between the passing of these two titans, Du Bois chaired the meeting in Fort Erie, Canada, that founded the Niagara Movement, later to become the National Association for the Advancement of Colored People (NAACP).

From the origin of the NAACP in 1909 until the early 1960s, its hegemony in the civil rights arena was unquestioned. It assumed and maintained its posture because of the association of such excellent men as Du Bois, Walter White, Mordecai Johnson, Charles Houston, Thurgood Marshall, Roy Wilkins, and Clarence Mitchell, to name a few.

Leadership defines that quality which inspires others to follow. In the Afro-American community the term has become a cliché, too often loosely used. Neither designation nor proclamation makes a leader. Yet just such attempts to drape the leadership toga around unworthy shoulders are incessantly underway.

Two essential functions of minority leadership are enlightenment and advocacy. Since the 1960s aspiring leaders have neglected to stir enlightenment into the brand of leadership they offered up. An engine is a necessary part of an automobile, but an engine is *not* an automobile. This vehicle requires, among other systems, a steering mechanism. A leader must offer guidance as well as motive power. This absence of enlightenment as a part of the leadership package is tragic because it is precisely the contingent of the Afro-American community most in need of enlightenment that is principally influenced by those who parade as leaders.

2. The Middle-class Afro-American

The middle-class Afro-American resonates to a greater or lesser degree with the vibrations of mainstream America. One or both parents in a family are gainfully employed, they have the education prerequisite for their jobs, and they own property or are in the process of becoming property owners. By virtue of their location in the middle stratum, they have the self-control and habits of mind that give their lives stability, and they have strategies for self-betterment that include themselves and especially their children. They arrived at their positions in life not through Headstart or any of the plethora of community-based programs and organizations that mushroomed during the last twenty years, but because they had the middle-class discernment to look and plan ahead. These parents instill their own values into their children—who, for the most part, are in schools or colleges appropriate to their ages.

The middle-class community is reasonably insulated from the influence of the fraudulently designated or self-proclaimed spokesmen who are only half-leaders, and more often than not, *mis*leaders.

3. The Coping Citizen

The contingent that manages to cope, the coping citizen or C-citizen, and the J-citizen (a designation to be explained later) represent different cases vis-à-vis the leadership humbuggery.

The C-citizen has survival instincts that lend him rudimentary viability in whatever environment he finds himself. He survives without thinking or planning. The maneuvers he needs to execute, and the moves he must or must not make, he finds self-evident. He cannot fathom the J-citizen's proclivity for false steps nor can he comprehend the sophisticated citizen's grotesque errors and lapses of judgment that so often cause his grand schemes to explode. The C-citizen is equally cognizant of the fallacies in minuscule or monumental magnitudes of nonsense, especially where they smack of innovation or adventurism.

C can be expected neither to improve his environment nor to be defeated by it. He is no more inventive than he is likely to go hungry. Depending upon where he first sees the light of day, C becomes a small farmer, miner, logger, common or semi-skilled laborer, salesman, or all of the above at one time or another. He engages in much the same type of employment as his father and expects his son to follow in his own honest, hardworking footsteps.

A casual encounter with the C-citizen reveals little difference between him and his middle-class counterpart. He is often found coping with life as well as the middle-classer does. At times when the middle-classer loses his footing in his obsession with future projections, C fares better. Nothing short of a perceptive scratch below the surface of C's psyche reveals the solitary quality that disqualifies him for the middle class. He is not future-focused. He is the quintessential "now" man—with the multiplicity of reflexes and traits that being "now" implies. His concerns are *pro tempore*. Despite his reasonably steady employment and income, he has no systematic savings program. He provides for his family on an incidental basis. The natural course of events finds his brood located in his abode, so he brings enough food from the market for everyone on deck. He is beset by such a clamor when they are out of shoes or clothing that appropriate purchases are made in the interest of diminishing the decibels. But innoculations and vaccinations, for example, are annoyances left to the school. Orthodontia and periodontia are literally Greek.

C's love is emotional rather than provident. He rends his garments in grief and recovers slowly, if ever, if per chance severe injury or death befalls one of his children. And he stands off a neighbor, a teacher, or a policeman whenever he perceives one of his offspring to be set upon, taking with alacrity whatever lumps accompany the effort. But, depending upon his mode of earning a livelihood, he eagerly anticipates the time when his children will be either of "some help" to him or "off his hands." He believes that a child should splash through a rudimentary education without becoming too saturated with learning or fancy ideas and get out into life "on his own" early on. C's father expected this of him and C passes the expectation along with a vengeance. He would never think of spending large sums of his hard-earned money on the education or training of a son as large or larger than himself, and who may eventually do better than he is doing and even "look down" on him. And as for a daughter, who in his right mind would throw education money away on someone equipped by nature to cope?

C is a firm believer in having "fun." His sole justification for exerting effort, beyond that which subsistence necessitates, is "fun." His impetus for seeking his first job, only months up from puberty, was not his father's scowls and glares and grunts of exasperation when C reached for a third helping at the supper table, but his own desire to have money to pay his fare into the circle of older boys who were obviously having so much fun. Without the disciplining whiplash of culturally induced long-range goals, who could resist the primeval-technological attraction of Jezebels, jazz, and jalopies?

The work-fun *modus vivendi* to which C's first job gives him the key never changes throughout his life. In time his family "happens" spontaneously and randomly, and the wheels of his existence spin out their prescribed circle. The children arrive unplanned, grow up tolerated, and, in their turn, are imbued with their ancestral capacity for coping.

C's existence is neither a happy nor an unhappy one. He is not contemplative. He surrenders what he must of his earnings to keep his spouse and brood off his neck, and the rest goes into outside activities.

Once his horizon expands beyond his original post-pubic pre-occupation, C settles into the comfortable armchair of spectator sports. He frequently invests a great deal of intellectuality in team scores and percentages and tactics and strategy; often becoming a flawless juggler of hundreds of names, averages, ratings, salaries, and individual exploits. An equal depth of understanding of valences, bonds, and atomic weights and numbers, with a smidgen of additional intellectual belt-tightening, would insure a baccalaureate in chemistry—the very thought of which would lay a wound across his cerebrum.

In the event C has an athletically talented son, C then becomes a great booster of the Little League, the junior high rollers, the varsity, or whatever. He whoops it up at practice and games, promotes family fun nights at the gymnasium, the stadium, the track, or ringside, and he boasts and breast-beats ad nauseam.

If the matter of savings ever crosses his mind, it is for the short-range accumulation of a down payment on some luxury item he has seen advertised, and whose ownership is either an indulgence or a symbol whose possession he thinks bestows the class he perceives in the ad model. It never occurs to C that the model portrays a lifestyle already in place before the product in question is acquired. C's sense of values and habits of mind blind him to the elaborate care given to exhibit the item, not as a luxury, but as a logical extension of the environment as staged.

C is only one atomic ring removed from middle class. One proper charge of intellectual electricity would give him that quantum jump upward to a controlled, focused, future-oriented outlook. And a concerned and discerning leadership would make the most of the opportunity. But the post-1960s spokesmen circulating in C's churches and schools and clubs flatter and fawn over him, praising him for his material well-being, while collecting money for additional boys' clubs and still more playground equipment.

4. The Jive Citizen

The word *jive* originated in the funky, smoky, noisy, drug-ridden underground dens of the early jazz musicians. It defined the free-rein improvisation on legitimate musical chords. It articulated the exuberance derived from thumbing one's nose at structure. And in time it gravitated into the Afro-American community.

The middle-class citizen recognized and accepted jive for what it was: an aberration from reality to be indulged in on red-letter days for short, rebellious interludes of freedom from the straitjacket of daily struggle. The C-citizen welcomed jive to the bar during his happy hours but strictly forbade the presence of the interloper in his work environment. But the contingent of the Afro-American community living permanently on the border of disarray accepted jive as its own. They refined jive. And in its refined state jive becomes disingenuous. In communications, both the jiver and its recipient recognize its basic mendacity but enjoy the perverted compliment and ego-stroking it lavishes. When jive becomes the primary mode of communication within a close subculture, it distorts reality. And citizens who communicate primarily in jive become Jive citizens, or J-citizens.

An illuminating insight into the J-youth's pathetic sense of values and aspirations is the scene played out hundreds of times on community playgrounds across the country every year during the autumn and into the winter. Kids in their early and middle teens, weighing barely a hundred pounds, are out in earnest pursuit of football prowess.

They envision themselves in highly paid professional roles and as autograph-signing television stars. They jive themselves blind to the fact that the youngsters who actually have a chance in the arena already weigh 180 pounds and upward.

This doomed army of youngsters nursing an impossible dream represents only the tip of the iceberg of the J-youth's problems. The assumption that fame and fortune are a mere hop and a skip down the road narrows their concentration to a single throw of the dice. The half-hearted effort put into school work prior to the athletic obsession stops completely. Then, when the bubble bursts, despair is inevitable. And out of the despair of the formative years comes the inevitable catalogue of anti-social attitudes. The J-youth thinks: "Life is unfair, the 'system' is all jive, society's rules are stacked against us, effort is futile, love is stillborn, hope is an illusion, and those who have even the most modest possessions are either lucky or thieves and deserve to have the tables turned on them."

The scenario plays with nauseating monotony. A leadership worthy of its name would comprehend that the deadly cycle needs interrupting. The J-youth should be offered a variety of pursuits early on, some of them maybe even mind expanding—something as exotic as, perhaps, a good book club, a mathematics society, a debating forum, or a chess divan. But what does the post-1965 spokesman offer? The usual mind-dulling panacea—additional playgrounds and better athletic equipment.

When the spokesmen are on a really cerebral binge they recommend community development programs—such as dance clubs, bong-bong bands, and little theatre groups—that vaguely hint at the possibility of being discovered for television and moving on to instant fame: Something in line with the J-youth's culturally induced delusion of the lucky strike and the big score.

5. When Leadership Lost its Way

It was in the 1960s that the Afro-American leadership first foreswore two of the most rudimentary ingredients necessary to the enlightenment of their constituency. The need for the ingredients is so obvious that they have been taken for granted throughout the struggle for Negro rights. The 1960s leaders first became mere spokesmen when they ceased to set examples of good manners and an agreeable personal appearance.

The dress code was derailed during the years when the students, both black and white, dropped out of colleges to forage through the deep South, instructing sharecroppers and day laborers in the arts and mechanics of voter registration. The young people risked their lives to hold clandestine rallies, meetings, and clinics. They gave impromptu seminars in local political science and hard-scrabble home economics by lamplight in isolated shacks—often only a jump ahead of the mob, or the sheriff and *his* mob—on lonely country roads in the darkness. Some were injured, a few murdered. But they persevered and raised the conscience of the country and the resolve of the disenfranchised until the entire nation became sufficiently aroused to demand the Civil Rights Act of 1964.

In the meantime the crusaders, young and idealistic and impressionable despite their sophisticated pretensions, were enchanted by what they perceived to be the spiritual purity of the victimized. They began emulating the mannerisms and style of dress of those whose freedom they were attempting to engineer. On their fund-raising dashes into the North they wore the farmhand's denim work uniform topped off with the regimental insignia of a thick head of carefully premeditated untrimmed and uncombed hair.

The fund-raisers began as emotional, semi-religious rituals in the hot, crowded living rooms of neighborhood sympathizers and in small churches with well-wishing congregations. Before long they became newsworthy and moved into larger churches and auditoriums. In the glow of the klieg lights, the appeals escalated to demands and the appealers with the greatest stage presence and fervor became media stars and, in some cases, demagogues. And gone as quickly as a whiff of perfume from a closing elevator door were the traditionally pressed suits and clean shirts and ties that had been the civil rights leadership uniform since John Russwurm and Frederick Douglass, since the days of Booker T. Washington's proper business-and-professional-man's attire and the scholarly elegance of William Du Bois. Gone were the care and pride in appearance that characterized the times of the NAACP's legal victories and the era of the freshly scrubbed faces, neat hairtrims, and laundered shirts and dresses of the sit-inners and freedom riders.

If one factors out the responsibility they should have felt for their emerging roles and the history and traditions of the civil rights struggle, it is difficult to condemn the young demagogues too seriously. More experienced and tempered personalities than they have been thrown off their stride by flashbulbs and interviews and instant celebrity status. It is not difficult, however, to recognize the serious seeds of mischief they sowed. And although the frenzied activity demanded by their cause left little time for reflection, most of them had, after all, been enrolled in colleges. Society expects a minimal level of ratiocination from beneficiaries of its institutions of higher learning. Somewhere in the recesses of their minds should have been embedded the idea that workable social processes and customs are chiefly those which have filtered downward and become refined through use by successive generations, usually arbitrated by the gifted of the lineage. This process precludes adopting the entire lifestyle of the unwashed masses at any given time as the *modus operandi* for progress. "A little child shall lead them" was proclaimed in reference to blind faith, not to intelligent action. And a belief that the unlettered and dis-advantaged could be the *arbiter elegantiae* of manners and style por-tends a disastrous blueprint for conduct.

When hints were dropped from the civil rights establishment that leadership protocol provided for neater dress and a less offensive mien, the response was immediate and shrill and contemptuous. The demagogues snapped back, via the media, of course, for all and sundry to hear, that if bringing the manners and dress and justifiable rage of the black field hands and day laborers to center stage was offensive, then offense was in. Reason was out. Had the old guard known their business and had any backbone, the last hundred years in the rights arena would not have been wasted. The current civil rights knights could have been in college pursuing their education instead of risking their necks on the hostile back-roads of the South, as the present state of civil rights required. The torch had been passed to the black activists under thirty, preferably eight to ten years under thirty, and the time for legal dillydallying and negotiations had passed. The time for having good manners like the house "darky" and wearing a tie and a hairtrim like the (white) "man" was passe.

Seeing themselves on the evening news after taping television interviews earlier in the day was heady stuff for the young Afro-American spokesmen. They were more impressed with their notoriety than if it had been prominence. In fact, any difference between the two escaped their discernment. There they were enjoying equal exposure with presidents, congressmen, cabinet members, and famous athletes, all without ever having paid their dues in the sense that the others arrived only after lifetimes of study and work and waiting. The *nouveau* leaders had arrived by simply "doing their thing"— speaking for their unfortunate brothers whom the system had kept unlettered and instilled with the fear of God, and, more satisfying, rebuking the civil rights Neanderthals and tongue-lashing the "man."

6. Redefining the Race

Intoxicated with their images and rhetoric, the demagogues outdid themselves on succeeding days to escalate the stridence and nonsense. Every mode of interface and accommodation ever worked out between the races was roundly denounced. The relationships were either servile and craven or beastly and exploitative. The Afro-American community discovered on the six o'clock news one evening that it was no longer Negro or colored, but "black." It no longer consisted of a community whose bloodlines ranged from 100 percent to less than 1.5 percent African. The community was now homogeneously black. Black had nothing to do with racial admixture or hue, the Afro-American community was told; it was a state of mind, a unifying force needed to resist racism. Besides, the presence of the rapist "beast's" blood in one's veins was something to be ashamed of at any rate, to be denied even in the face of overwhelming evidence to the contrary.

Many middle-class Afro-Americans over thirty years of age, hundreds of whom fell short of being pure black by various sums of various powers of one-half, were uneasy about the new designation and the unbridled stridence. Their lives had been ordered, sometimes for two or three generations, and it had never occurred to them that they should be ashamed of who they were. Many were even proud of their biracial and sometimes triracial lineages, and of the strides they had made under trying circumstances. So, to learn suddenly, out of the mouths of babes, that the only thing in their lives worthy of pride was their black blood was more than a little unsettling. But even stronger than their dismay at the new label, given the country's racist tradition, was their reluctance to speak out in such a way that, in the charged atmosphere at the time, might be construed as opposition to unity against racism. So they maintained an uneasy silence. Besides, the demagogues had a hammerlock on the media.

The media loved every moment of the demagogues' shenanigans. The youth were articulate, brash, reckless, controversial, and on the attack. According to their lights, "black" rang out just the right combination of innovation and defiance. It represented a much-needed new focus on the racial problem, and it took a word that had heretofore been insulting and demeaning and turned it around. It confronted the insult head-on. It patently rejected the long-standing definition of what was good and what was bad, what was virtuous and what was evil. Since the "man" was immoral, xenophobic, and autotheistic, he was blinded, and his assessments were *ipso facto* incorrect. So they boldly set about to recast the meaning of the language of the time.

The "black" designation stuck like chewing gum on wool. It played to the public's penchant for contrasts and simplistic labels. Now an individual was clearly either black or white. It also cleared up a serious problem with which many whites had wrestled over the years: They had never been quite sure whether to address an Afro-American with whom they wanted good relations as "Negro" or "colored." Up to that point "black" had been out. It had been an opprobrium. Now the answer was simple. For the whites who had always preferred to think of the Afro-American as black, not quite American, and, as a group, to be lumped into one easily defined and somewhat derogatory category, it had at long last become legitimate for them to have their cake and eat it, too.

Just about everyone was ready for the "black" label but the middle-class, over-thirty Afro-American. *Black* is an absolute word like *clear* and *pure* and *pregnant* and *dead* and, yes, like *white*. No one asks about the various shades of black as one does about the shades of red and green and happy. So, as such, "black" is inaccurate as a racial or color designation for more than 73 percent of the Afro-

American population. But the inaccuracy is the least of its objectionable features. In the Judeo-Christian world the word *black* had a black eye before English was a written language. The heavenly robe and the bridal gown have been white to define purity and virtue and perfection down through the ages. The center of power and symbol of continuity in the United States is the White House. The good guys wear white hats and a harmless spoof is a white lie. In contrast, "black" has always implied just the opposite. It has been synonymous with evil and sin and mystery. Since time out of mind there have been blackguard language and conduct, blackhearted deeds, black art, black cats (and bad luck), the Black Death, and heinous crimes suitably committed in the black of night.

A flesh-crawling horror of the blackness of night is genetic in northern peoples. It is not for nothing that Christmas, the principal Western holiday, comes in the last week of December. Eons before Christianity superimposed Christ's birthday anniversary over the festival, northern pagans observed the passing of the longest and blackest night of the year in a dithyrambic celebration of the winter solstice.

The youths who elected to designate themselves and their constituency with a word so laden with negativism were more brash than observant. They were more articulate than cognitive, and had more affrontery than historical perspective. If they thought they could alter the impact that an age-old word has on the community thought process with the force of a righteous snarl on the evening news, they stand commended for their courage but condemned for their judgment. And contrary to their cocksure contention that "Negro" was a racist-coined putdown, the word is as old as the Greek language. More than five hundred years before Christ, *piper nigrum* imported from India was used, not as a condiment but a valuable medicine, in Athens and environs. It is unlikely that the pepper's description was a derogatory one.

Once "black" was legitimized, a grab bag of additional propositions were put forward in an ever-increasing crescendo of babble. No notion, no matter how incomplete or poorly thought out, was withheld. Whatever popped into the demagogues' heads popped out of their mouths. They turned on the colleges and universities with a vengeance, these being the culprits who had suppressed and misrepresented black contributions to culture and history and deliberately cast blacks in a bad light.

When the universities conceded the possibility of some truth in the charges and asked for suggestions, the demagogues reacted with screams of rage rather than gestures of cooperation. They thumbed their noses at conferences. Whatever they had to say was for public consumption, preferably via television. "Working quietly behind the scenes," was spat out in derision as the technique of the "Tom."

The demagogues demanded courses in black history, black music, black culture, and Swahili. In addition they screamed for autonomous black studies departments and all-black dormitories.

When the question arose as to why black dormitories, since it had been thought that the point of the struggle was desegregation, the demagogues answered that they had changed their minds. Advanced-thinking blacks like themselves were in a better position to lead other blacks than anyone else.

By the time the black studies departments and black dormitories were on the road to implementation, the scream went up for reparations—for four hundred years of injustice. And as unbelievable as it may seem, there were major church denominations who actually took the demands seriously and entered into concrete negotiations to pay. In the meantime, other demagogues were demanding the right to carry guns in the classroom and on airplanes—to protect themselves from the "man."

In time the charade began to assume the aspects of a ghetto carnival of hell-raising and hustling. None of the demagogues ever settled down to serious study—of black studies or of anything else. And as far as anyone is able to ascertain, none ever learned Swahili. And what if they had? Who ever heard of a Swahili rocket, a Swahili refrigerator, a Swahili radio, or even a Swahili wheel? The language would be of no use in the Atlantic community.

In the final analysis, studying Swahili was as hare-brained as most of the other demagogic ideas. And it was good riddance when the media tired of their cacophony and found other sources of sensationalism. The demagogues did leave a legacy, unfortunately— one of negativism and erroneous concepts, the ills of which succeeding leadership aspirants are still suffering.

7. Early Trailblazers

The demagogues and their true-believing adherents were thoroughly self-righteous and arrogant. They boasted and blustered and banged the tables impatiently in their strategy meetings. And the way they scoffed at any suggestions of temperance clearly indicated that they thought themselves the inventors of rebellion against racism. Biblio-phobes that they were, they failed to recognize that historically they were positioned near the tail end of a very difficult but typically American evolutionary process. The Negro rebellion had begun more than a hundred years before the birth of the Republic and continued unrelentingly throughout every succeeding decade. It had taken innumerable twists and turns and received assistance from equally innumerable and sometimes equally unlikely quarters. Any chronicle of racial progress in America will provide a catalogue of events of which the following are among the highlights:

Not twenty years before the decade of the demagogues, Jackie Robinson became the first Negro to play in professional baseball. By the 1960s an Afro-American in baseball, or any other sport, was "no big thing." But Robinson was carefully chosen by Branch Rickey, manager of the Brooklyn Dodgers, as he had to be in vie· of race relations at the time. Robinson was educated, and possessed an impressive bearing, exemplary self-control, and outstanding athletic ability. Prior to his entry on the scene, there had been no nationally popular integrated professional teams. And misgivings had abounded concerning public acceptance, fan loyalty, and player hostility. They all reared their ugly heads, but Robinson rode out the storm with courage and self-control. He was a trailblazer, and by the time he left the diamond, the American public was becoming accustomed to seeing Negroes participating in mainstream activities. This public perception of Afro-Americans "belonging" was an absolute prerequisite to the civil rights advances that followed.

Also in the decade of Robinson's entry into big league baseball in the 1940s, James Farmer had led an integrated group of his associates into segregated restaurants and theatres and had tested recently passed regulations in interstate travel. At that time such rebellious activity was extremely dangerous and required a great deal of courage and savvy. Civil rights activists were anything but the darlings of the media in that era.

Little more than five years prior to Farmer's introduction of nonviolent direct action into the civil rights arena, in 1935, Thurgood Marshall returned to the University of Maryland Law School. Five years earlier he had been barred from enrolling there because of his race. This time, with the blessings of the Maryland Court of Appeals, before which he had argued *Murray v. State of Maryland,* Marshall installed Donald Murray as a student there.

In 1905, thirty years before Marshall and Murray, William Du Bois had felt the need to cross the border to Fort Erie, Canada, to organize the Niagara Movement. The Movement's purpose was aggressive action on behalf of Negro rights. The organization was so well launched that within nine years it had evolved into the NAACP.

Thirty-three years farther back in the annals of history, in 1872, Booker T. Washington left central West Virginia, when the state was only nine years old. He walked and hitched rides on ox carts and wagons to the Atlantic coast of Virginia to apply for entrance at Hampton Institute. The sixteen-year-old Washington spent weeks following poorly marked mountain trails through the Appalachians, sleeping in the open as often as inside some good Samaritan mountaineer's cabin or barn—this at a time when wolves and panthers were as prevalent in that part of the country as poodles are today in Central Park in summer. And equally dangerous were the xenophobic hillbillies isolated in the woods and hollows, and the defeated planters and small landholders in the Piedmont, who were still picking at their wounds with fingernails of rage over having lost the Civil War. To say that Booker navigated a hostile landscape is a classic understatement.

In 1859, thirteen years prior to Washington's trek, John Brown, after underground railroading in Massachusetts and jayhawking in Kansas, maintained his single-minded dedication to manumission and hallowed the ground with his smoking rifle and martyr's death at Harper's Ferry.

Ten years before John Brown at Harper's Ferry and 105 years before Thurgood Marshall argued Linda Brown before the Warren Court, in 1849 Charles Sumner escorted Sarah Roberts to a segregated school in Boston. In *Roberts v. City of Boston,* Sumner became the first lawyer to introduce the then-unheard-of concept of equal protection under the law for Negroes.

Fifteen years prior to Sumner and Roberts, in 1834 Frederick Douglass turned on the professional slave breaker to whom he had been consigned as a spirited young buck. Douglass administered a thorough beating to his warden—literally breaking the slave breaker. And four years later he escaped to launch his distinguished career as one of the spokesmen for several anti-slavery societies in New England.

Only three years before Douglass made his violent move, Nat Turner made an even more far-reaching one. In 1931, he organized and led the most successful guerrilla rampage ever mounted in the Western hemisphere by any slave except Toussaint L'Ouverture of Haiti. He assaulted life and property with such fury for about twenty-four hours in Southampton County, Virginia, that shock waves of terror richocheted through every nook and cranny of the slavocracy long after Turner had been caught and killed. After Turner, sensitive Southerners knew viscerally that the institution of slavery was no longer viable. Its end was no longer a matter of if, but of how and when.

In 1800, thirty-one years before Nat Turner and a century and two-thirds before the media manufactured demagogues, Gabriel Prosser and Denmark Vesey entered their names in the historical records of Virginia and South Carolina, respectively. Both organized vast plots to capture the major cities of their states: Prosser at Richmond and Vesey at Charleston. Both were betrayed at the last minute, however. Prosser and Vesey paid with their lives, but not before they laid to rest the slaveocracy's propaganda about the happy, docile slave dancing a jig under the magnolia tree in the moonlight after having worked sixteen hours in the field.

Back more than a quarter of a century prior to Prosser and Vesey, and during the birth throes of the Republic, Benjamin Franklin and Thomas Jefferson coerced the Continental Congress into promising to bar the importation of slaves after the end of 1775. The Congress later reneged on its promise, in part because including the provision would have fractured the Republic into tiny countries after the fashion of Western Europe. However, Franklin and Jefferson never changed their minds and continued to press their case. And thirty-three years later, after Franklin's death, the slave trade was outlawed. The effect of the 1808 legislation was *de jure* rather than *de facto,* however. But its tardiness and sham in no way reduced the stature of Franklin and Jefferson.

As far back as 1663 a far-reaching slave revolt took place in Virginia. And spanning the two hundred years between 1663 and 1863, more than 250 revolts were recorded, and perhaps as many unrecorded ones took place with clockwork regularity.

8. Rebellion in Evolution

Rebellions are as old as repression, which, in turn, is older than civilization. And the spirit of rebellion lives on even when the uprising itself is stamped into the ground. Consequently, rebellions rise up out of the very dust again and again. The hope for freedom and justice springs eternal in the human breast.

The Afro-American rebellion against slavery and second-class citizenship was an ongoing activity. It flared up randomly and regularly throughout the length and breadth of the land and manifested itself in every imaginable form. The methods ranged from riots to rallies, and from negotiations to court cases to the publication of newspapers.

It was through their newspapers that the Afro-American developed a sense of community. Cohesion was a long time in coming because it was predicated on a substantial level of literacy, and the constituency was spread over more than three and a half million square miles. In time, however, a sufficient number of little red school houses, both missionary and public, were put in place, a rudimentary literacy was achieved, and the sense of community accrued.

In the meantime some of the little school houses were becoming bigger. Students were beginning to enroll and graduate from the few colleges and the two or three available schools of medicine and law. Some of the more ambitious students of the law school were sharpening their skill sufficiently to cope with America's mainstream counselors. And since the United States government is one of laws, fittingly, it was through the Afro-American's own effort in the courts of law at this juncture in the development of his education that he first saw the cracks of daylight in the walls of segregation.

This observation is not intended to imply that Afro-Americans were not represented in the courts on "rights" issues before Afro-American lawyers learned the ropes. After all, Charles Sumner's representation of Sarah Roberts in Boston came twenty years before the enactment of the Fourteenth Amendment, and was only one of a long list of such cases. It is important, however, to observe that, except in a few instances, mainstream lawyers brought the proper spirit and motivation to the cases they represented but not always the fervor and do-or-die attitude that the Negro lawyers brought. And even more significant, it was impossible to imagine the courts taking the litigation on behalf of an ethnic group too seriously when that group was incapable of assuming responsibility for its own welfare.

Once Negro lawyers assumed the legal responsibility, the mainstream press began to take Afro-American complaints seriously. When an aggrieved citizen sued a political jurisdiction for misconduct, the event became newsworthy. The metropolitan newspapers of the land carried the stories; the pros and cons of the cases came up for debate; and editorial comment often favored the aggrieved minority. The process fostered a climate of expectation in the black community.

It was in such a climate that the students in Greensboro sat at a "white" lunch counter in 1960 and refused to move when told to do so by the store manager. At any time prior to the stance for decency taken by the courts and the press, the students would have had their heads bashed in and would have been thrown in jail (if not the gutter) and forgotten about.

What really tipped the scales in favor of the Greensboro students, the hundreds of other students, and the hordes of older people who followed them, was the television camera—the ultimate communications machine. No longer could the national government, the power brokers, the religious and moral leaders, nor even the average decent-minded citizen pretend not to know or believe the stories about the barbarity practiced against their Afro-American countrymen. There, in full color, before them day after day was the spectacle of clubs, cattle prods, and fire hoses, used by the faces of meanness incarnate, on Negro citizens who were merely attempting to exercise the prerogatives that other citizens in Western Christiandom took for granted. Corrective steps were obviously in order, from many quarters and for a number of reasons. First, there was the role of the federal government. The nation had fought two world wars at the sacrifice of the lives of thousands of its youth and the not-so-young to defend freedom around the globe. It had recast governments in Europe and Asia in the name of individual liberty. It had intervened in what it chose to call repressive regimes throughout Central and South America in the name of *vox populi,* and trumpeted self-righteously before the world about the correctness of its cause. America had brooked no repression of liberty in the Western hemisphere. Now it stood exposed *flagrante delicto,* permitting one group of citizens in its southern states to deny another group the rights it had been espousing since before the Boston Tea Party. Second, there were the religious and moral leaders. They had ever waxed eloquent, both oratorically and literally, in the name of God and country and common decency, on the sacrosanctity of freedom and liberty. Now, in view of the panorama of carnage taking place before their very eyes on the television screens, they realized that addressing specifics rather than broad generalities was urgently in order. And finally, there were the sensitivities of the ordinary citizens. They had wanted to believe the cozy little platitudes they had always heard about the warm, paternal, and mutually beneficial relations between the races in the South. Now they looked at their televisions and beheld a lot of suffering. Somewhere below the threshold of their consciousness they realized that there, but for the racial buffers and the grace of God, go we. And they felt a little sick and cynical about some of their national totems supposedly erected to liberty.

In the final analysis then, it was the high level of communications technology, rather than any change in the nature of the personalities involved, that dictated the ultimate outcome of the Negro rebellion of the 1960s. It was time-dependent and therefore evolutionary rather than revolutionary.

9. The New Restraint in Law Enforcement

Massive outbursts of social energy, like enormous weather disturbances, usually recontour the landscape. Some of the alterations are immediately recognizable improvements, others require becoming accustomed to.

The southern law enforcement agencies' reaction to the sit-ins, freedom rides, and marches enraged the Afro-American masses. The inner-city youth in many of the country's metropolitan areas went on rampages of rioting and looting and burning. The first burning binge occurred in 1965 in the Watts section of Los Angeles. It represented a colossal outburst of pent-up rage. Hundreds of stores and dwellings were burned to the ground, and sporting goods establishments and pawnshops were looted for guns and ammunition. The rioting lasted seven days.

The local and federal law enforcement agencies had one of two choices: They could stamp out the disorder with force, or employ restraint and contain the fury within its perimeters until it spent itself. They chose restraint. In earlier days the constabulary would have entered and suppressed the lawlessness with ruthless enthusiasm. But in Watts the fury had so much momentum that restoring order would have required slaughtering vast numbers of Afro-Americans and laying another disfiguring wound across the "face of freedom" before the omnipresent television cameras. The index pointing toward restraint had been pre-selected at any rate. In the climate generated by the recent southern confrontations, the federal government had begun to enter the fray on the side of the Afro-American cause. To enter the perimeter of the Watts conflagration in a hard-nosed stance would have been a confusing reversal of its role.

Once it became apparent that law enforcement had assumed a greatly restrained posture, a long series of rampages went off like a chain of firecrackers on Independence Day. The ghetto youth missed the import of the police restraint. Since the government had not moved with resolve to build equality into the political and educational systems until the confrontations and riots were underway, the demagogues were left with the impression that they had frightened the government into action. Unaware of such nuances as national image, world opinion, credibility, and endogenous sensibilities as they were, it became apparent to the untried, untempered youngsters that the way to acquire one's dues was to raise hell. It was equally apparent that what the demagogues had maintained all along was in fact true. Good manners and reasonableness and a neat appearance were irrelevant to the acquisition of what one wanted. So up went the raised fist brandishing in cadence with bellows of "black power."

10. The New Irrelevancies

Once the young demagogues began weaving their patchwork of irrelevancies, their contentions were as extremist as their demands for bearing arms and forming autonomous black studies departments in major universities. They maintained their proposition that the poverty-stricken field hand and sharecropper constituted the "salt of the earth." To these two categories they now added the urban J-citizen. After all, J was in the front lines of the successful rioting and looting campaigns. So the worldview of the field hand, sharecropper, and Jive citizen, with minor modifications, dictated the directions to be struck out upon by the "New Black Joe and Jane."

Anything considered worthy by the "man," or deemed beneficial to the "system," or approved by the former civil rights grandees or even the middle-class Afro-American—now contemptuously referred to as the "Establishment Black"—was put on the index of irrelevancies.

The list was as interesting as it was incredulous to everyone except its perpetrators and the C and J communities. One could never quite believe that all the perpetrators of the fraudulent list were themselves thoroughly convinced. A few had bachelor's degrees and, now and then, someone with an advanced degree surfaced in their midst. The entire thrust gave off the unhealthy effluvium of either crass opportunism or *dementia praecox.*

Education posed a serious problem for the demagogues. According to their lights, schools gave everything a racist slant and diabolically omitted anything edifying or relevant to black people. Besides, it seemed that a year of rioting and defiance had achieved more than a century of education and training and good citizenship.

If learning to read, write, and speak correctly and to use fractions, decimals, percentages, and more required systematic self-effacement, then these pursuits would have to be thrown out with the more blatant subjects like geography, history, and the other social sciences. Besides, they argued, black students should be concentrating on Swahili rather than English anyway. And woe unto the puzzled young recidivist who screwed up enough courage occasionally to respectfully inquire if there were not a smidgen of value in knowing how to read a want ad, write a resumé, speak correct English during an interview, understand credit financing, or even calculate the voltage drop across a Wheatstone bridge. The high priests of blackdom ridiculed him as Exhibit One of system sophistry, seeing him as one who had been deceived about the proper order of black priorities, and as one who stood in desperate need of the "new black orientation."

English, mathematics, chemistry, biology, as well as history and economics, were declared irrelevant to the black position vis-à-vis the system. Those subjects were for people whose identities, sanity, and lives and limbs were secure—dilettantes who had the leisure to devote to non-gritty diversions. Besides, slogging through the ooze of such beastly abstractions required an unwarranted amount of toil and discipline and precision. That in itself was a form of slavery and was thus unbecoming of the new free, self-respecting black. So the word from the demagogues was, "Down with form and discipline and mental drudgery, and up with free-form rapping and ranting and chanting"—the new education according to the new black metaphysic.

Another of the curious propositions propounded by the black ideologues had to do with the separation of middle-class Afro-American teenagers from the influence of their homes and families. The theory held that traditional education, the work ethic, and a future orientation adversely affected the outlook of the new black citizen and handicapped him for the role he was destined to play in the new society under development.

The pied pipers of blackdom had a great deal of influence. To a teenager experimenting with methods of rebelling against parental authority during those years, a demagogue only a few seasons his senior telling off the whole country on television was the embodiment of heroism. More middle-class youngsters than one likes to remember broke loose from the family moorings and gave themselves over to the new monomania.

It was a tragedy of United States history that, at the very moment when equal opportunity became available to the Afro-American after scores of years of having been subtended within the narrow arc of inequality, there had been a rapacious changing of the leadership guard, and the new spokesmen were not ready. They were floundering about in a dense fog of idealism, egotism, and revenge. Having inverted the aphorism, "might makes right," to the assertion that "deprivation and ignorance are the parents of spiritual purity," they were hell-bent on glorifying the culture of the loser. Intoxicated with the media interpretation of the roles they had played in the recent social changes, they had no intention of desisting from the frenzy of activity that accompanied the party. No thought was given to formulating plans for solidifying their gains. To an individual, they wanted more and still more action and media exposure. The role rather than the results had become their *raison d'être*.

To keep up the momentum of attack that had brought their days of glory, additional wrongs and slights inflicted on their constituency had to be unearthed. Where there were no wrongs, rights had to be reinterpreted to appear wrong. The demagogues became expert at racial mind reading and concentrating on the ills of society, even when it required extrapolating "four hundred years" backward into history. It never occurred to them to advocate grasping the horns of the new opportunities that abounded, especially where the grasping required preparation. They preferred nursing a grudge to self-betterment.

11. Unrecognized Relevancies

The pathetic leadership predicament of the last two decades produced no one to counsel young C and J against nursing delusions of grandeur. It is a common occurrence to hear students in the corridors of inner-city high schools confidently projecting that within the next few years they will have positions paying multiples of the national median annual salary and many more times the median salary of Afro-Americans. And they are speaking in all sincerity. Specific questioning reveals that they have no concept of the nature and depth of skills that warrant the ambitious salaries they have in mind. They entertain vague notions about sitting at executive desks and making important decisions, not realizing that compensation levels are based on the degree of esteem society has for one's skills and talents and experience. Their ignorance of the prerequisites for grand salaries is usually reflected in the shallow education they exhibit, and their fantasies are expressed in atrocious English and ghetto clichés.

C and J children come by their life experiences in reverse order. They learn that there is no Santa Claus before they become old enough to experience the magical anticipation of Christmas. They learn cynicism before courtesy, and cynicism slows learning to a painful and practically useless crawl. Not much of a paragraph of reading is absorbed when the reader's mind is busy questioning the motives and authenticity of the writer. The preponderance of learning takes place at the stage in life when one soaks up the facts and precepts around him without question. Within reason, the longer one believes that his environment is forthright and just and that it is functioning in his interest, the longer one is able to absorb knowledge rapidly.

Learning the alphabet would be next to impossible if a teacher were compelled to justify the reason why B rather than G, for example, follows A; or why X is made with two slanting lines rather than two lines that cross at 90 degrees, as in a "plus" sign. Learning the alphabet is neither the time nor the place for philosophizing and cynicism. One simply learns the names, shapes, and order of the symbols as they stand. Farther down the road, the multiplication tables are learned the same way. At the introductory stage, little consideration is given to why seven times eight equals fifty-six. It is simply a fact to be memorized so thoroughly that if one is awakened in the dead of night he can give the answer and never remember having been disturbed. Many abstruse observations accompany the multiplication of seven times eight. There are the commutative law, the series of additions concept, and numerous other applicable number theories. But when the argumentation and debate process is prematurely introduced into the curtain-raiser phase, trouble and confusion are introduced with it.

Some distance down the road beyond alphabetics and the multiplication tables, one encounters trigonometry. The length of the side opposite the central angle divided by the length of the radius vector of a right triangle inscribed in a unit circle is called the sine of the angle. The adjacent side over the radius vector is called the cosine, and so forth. There are six basic trigonometric functions to be memorized. If the class is to keep its momentum and cover the concepts of the course in the allotted time, no room is left for philosophy. No time is available to convince the teenaged cynic that the relationship of the sine to the cosecant is justified, or to persuade him that the cosecant should not be called, say, the recip-sine.

Even farther up the academic ladder, when assumptions and proofs have become part of the mathematics fare, students in many of the world's pressure-cooker engineering schools are required to commit large sections of the table of integrals to memory. There is not enough time to thumb through the tables to solve all the problems the students are required to solve. However, by this stage of the learning process, the students who were prematurely introduced to caviling, or who were permitted to do so, are light-years removed from the state of mental acuity that advanced inquiry demands.

Forcing a hard-nosed posture of inquiry on youngsters or permitting them to assume one before it develops naturally from an assembled store of facts imposes a dangerous learning imbalance upon them that they do not deserve. If they reverse the order of memorizing and questioning, chances are that the subtle distinctions between definitions, facts, and assumptions on the one hand, and postulates, theories, and logic on the other, will escape them thereafter. They will never know when to accept an idea, when to examine it, or when to question and require proof of it. The tragedy is that they are likely to remain forever deprived of the elevating ideas and insights floating like pretty pastel balloons just above their heads in the world's main current of civilization and enlightenment.

The demagogues missed the principle that relevance expands as one's horizons broaden. The alphabet is hardly relevant to pupils on their first day at school. But it becomes so as they concentrate on its structure and order. Later, reading becomes relevant also, after the mystery of stringing letters together clears up and the pupils perceive the new universe of stories, ideas, and directions available through the written word. Still later, pupils learn to apply arithmetic processes to grasp the concepts of measurements, ranges, dimensions, and amounts; then the multiplication tables, fractions, and decimals become relevant. Yet, the 1960s found scores of cavalier ignoramuses advising people even younger than themselves that subjects as important as history, anatomy, agriculture, geopolitics, differential equations, and the like were irrelevant. And their case has rested there—over much too wide an area—until this day.

12. Jive's One-way Cultural Filter

No spokesman has come center stage within the last two decades to point out to the C- and J-youth the difference between merely wishing for a commodity and doing something concrete about acquiring it. Going between points A and B, or setting about to acquire something one wants, seems simple enough to a practical individual in touch with the real world. The same trip poses an impossible navigational feat around the reefs and shoals of hardship and uncertainty for a youth born and bred behind the barricades of Jive. Having been christened and nourished on illusion, he knows nothing about the contours of reality outside his culture. If he appears alienated from the world beyond his ghetto, it is because he *is* an alien in the outside world. C and J feel helpless and frustrated because of their lack of the practical knowledge for acquiring the accoutrements that the advertisements indicate everyone deserves and everyone *else* has.

It is the meaning of *deserve* that throws J. The implication drawn from *deserve* in the mainstream world includes having worked, saved, planned, and waited until the time was right. For the Jive youth, *deserve* implies mere being. His environment teaches the "mere being" theory as thoroughly as the mainstream middle-class environment teaches systematic planning and working.

When J-youths dream of escaping their narrow surroundings, their musings are invariably woven around singing, dancing, acting, or playing their way out via the athletic route. These pursuits appear to be based upon physical endowment and luck. They are supposed to be fun, and are decidedly tilted toward the kinesthetic rather than the cognitive. These pursuits are especially attractive because they involve the element of chance; and the smaller the likelihood of their occurrence, the more exciting they are to contemplate. This is the cheap, pleasant mystique of Jive daydreams.

Jive culture—consisting as it does of an unhealthy admixture of emotionalism, superstition, fantasies, frustrations, and confusion—generates a great deal of heat and high-frequency oscillations. In an egalitarian society it radiates toward other cultures in its environs. While these other cultures have inter-cultural antennae and are able to receive the Jive messages, J-cultures only receive outside signals oscillating on a J-wavelength. As a result J lives within a one-way cultural filter. His messages are beamed outward but he gets nothing that lies outside his perimeter of experience in return. So, as a consequence of the implacable laws of physics and society, the influence goes the wrong way and imposes the rotten-apple syndrome in spades.

Many middle-class parents living within J's broadcast radius are jolted out of their minds. While they are attempting to instill forward-looking values and habits in their children, they see their offspring tipping their hats to Jivedom. The tug-of-war is dismaying and often a downright losing proposition in cases where the middle-class youngster is teetering between self-control on the one hand and sloth and frivolity on the other. The child who resents his parents as killjoys whose only pleasure is to see him suffering through the odious trials of homework, learning good hygienic and dietary habits, and keeping his activities organized and stabilized is seduced by the Jive community *modus vivendi*. It resembles the proverbial rat colony without the alpha male. There is a great deal of loafing and free play, and the lines of conduct are fuzzy to nonexistent. Early love and overt promiscuity are rampant. The general aimlessness and lack of restraint fascinates the outside observer who is fighting the reins of family discipline and order.

An obvious commentary on how the customs and attitudes of the J-culture renders its citizens unfit to interface with the outside community is the inordinate percentage of its male population found in jails. They run afoul of the law at an early age and spend most of their lives passing in and out of the criminal justice turnstile. Unfortunately, the spokesmen to whom they listen reinforce their contention that the "system" is out of step with them rather than the other way around.

13. Three-dimensional Common Sense

No spokesman has stood on the public podium within the last two decades to explain many of the how-tos that the C and J youth need to know. The post-1960s spokesmen are too preoccupied with their roles as advocates to become involved as mentors. Both roles are essential to ethnic leadership. There are times when one role is more important than the other. In the 1950s and early 1960s, advocacy was more important. It was obvious that the Afro-American deserved more participation in society's mainstream than either law or custom permitted. But in the 1970s, mentorship should have taken the front seat. The barriers to mainstream participation had been dismantled. Middle-class Afro-Americans were enjoying the advantages of American citizenship. Yet the J-citizen was no more involved in Americana in a mutually beneficial way than they were in the 1960s. The spokesmen to whom they looked for direction continued attacking rather than teaching.

The success of the advocates blinded the aspirant leaders who followed to the need of the mentor role. The new "leaders" have not discerned the difference between battlefield protocol and securing a foothold.

Whenever the current crop of spokesmen decide to caucus with their constituency, they do more listening than talking. The counselor who listens too sympathetically soon falls into the cant and thought patterns of those he sets out to aid, stumbling into the trap the young voter registrants fell into in the 1960s. In this instance the counselor is mistaking ignorance and arrogance for clairvoyance into the ills of society.

A leader of strength and vision realizes the need to establish the terms of his relationship with those he hopes to lead. He is assertive *with* the group as well as *for* the group. He is willing to listen and caucus, but the quality that makes a leader is not listening and conferring, but asserting leadership. The aspiring leaders of the post-1960s era have never gotten past the listening, groveling, mimicking stage. None have been forthright and presumptuous enough to talk three-dimensional common sense to C and J.

Three-dimensional common sense consists of what, how, and why. A first *what* gives a topic a point of departure, and succeeding *whats* can be made to draw a line of reasoning extending from the point. In a conversation with a junior high school student, for example, the following line could be drawn: What career are you planning to pursue? What courses do you need to get under way? What courses are you taking now? What is your aptitude for these courses? What makes you think you will be content in this career? What contribution do you expect to make to your family, community, and country in this career?

The first *how* could coincide with the first *what,* with succeeding *hows* stretching away in a line at 90 degrees with the *what* line: How did you happen to decide on this career? How long will it take you to prepare for it? How much will it cost? How do you plan to finance the cost? How does your counselor feel about your choice? How does your family feel?

The two lines determine a *what-how* plane as smooth as a large mirror lying face-up on the floor. Any legitimate *what* or *how* that comes to mind may be placed at a selected point in the plane for inspection, discussion, review, or reflection. A line of *whys* drawn perpendicular to the *what-how* plane will clarify the discussion further by giving it a third dimension. The questions could consist of: Why did you select this career from others so similar that seem to require about the same aptitudes and preparation? Why did you choose one that requires so much (so little) preparation? Why did you choose one so unlike (or similar to) the careers followed by other graduates of your school? Why do you think your parents will (or will not) help you?

These three mutually perpendicular lines of Socratic inquiry define a construction resembling a table-top aquarium. It has length and breadth and depth. It may be viewed from any angle and from any distance for perspective. The relationships between all the *whats, hows,* and *whys* can be easily assessed. The proposition has credibility because one sees one's world in three dimensions. The structure takes thought and planning and time, but no one with youthful imagination could leave the discussion of a vital concern with a flat, uninspired outlook. Not every C and J youth could be recovered with the use of such a construct, but given an early start and sustained effort, more would be saved than lost. Furthermore, the lines involving the discussion of a course of study could be applied to the discussion of a variety of subjects. Love, sex, marriage, parenting, employment, purchasing an automobile, and recreation are but a small sample.

One of a leader's functions is setting goals. Up until the 1960s a question sure to enter a conversation of any duration between a mature man and a pre-adolescent boy in the Afro-American community was, "What do you want to be when you grow up, son?" The child was in for a grave lecture if he mumbled, "I don't know," or worse yet, "Nothing." Of course, that was before the professors of education popularized the idea that the child is absolutely equal to the grownup except for size. The smaller copy has the same sensitivities, rights to privacy, rights of choice and decision, and right to express his inexperienced opinions and have them considered on an equal basis with those of experience. This includes the right to reject unsolicited advice. In addition, the child has a right to compensate for his lack of size by throwing temper tantrums and otherwise exercising bad manners and a bit of barbarism now and then.

One very basic *what* has to do with a young person's use of his time. What about the interval between the end of the school day and bedtime? Should it be spent at the playground or before the television? A thoughtful mentor could spell out its proper use.

People are respected and paid according to the rung they occupy on the "ladder of service" they provide their communities. The services may range from the essential to the important to the frivolous. But the services define the activities for which the community is willing to pay. There are as many ladders of service as there are professions and trades to ply, and more new ones arise or are invented than disappear each day. There is always at least one "ladder of service" that any individual can climb. Finding it is simply a matter of searching persistently or having the proper guidance.

Once the ladder is found, the rung one occupies on it depends upon how he spent his time on the rung immediately below. Therefore youngsters must be instructed in the techniques of ascending from rung to rung. They must be provided with the manual on developing study habits, using their mental faculties, and learning to live comfortably with schedules and guidelines and deadlines. Once these skills are mastered, succeeding rungs upward become easier. The height at which one settles depends largely on his concentration and energy and ambition. These precepts are practically absorbed by osmosis in middle-class cultures. They are not endogenous to the C and J cultures, however, so it is incumbent upon contemporary spokesmen to point up the *whats* and to supply the *hows* and *whys* to C and J.

A low expectation quotient has been diagnosed as one of the more serious ills of the black ghetto. Expectation consists of a complex admixture—part learned and part discovered. The learned and discovered aspects of a reasonable expectation wax when an individual has a three-dimensional view of an obtainable goal.

The child of middle-class professional parents, living and attending school in a homogeneous neighborhood, expects to become a professional. His speech habits, thought patterns, viewpoints, and study routines all condition him for a professional life. The question is not whether he is going to college, but where he is going to college.

The youngster in the Jive culture has some vague and ill-defined expectation of "making it" in the streets. This means a little gambling, a little confidence gaming, and a little racketeering if the opportunity arises. Then there is a little welfare, or a catch-as-catch-can job now and then, when all else fails. Needless to say, all the youngster's language habits, thought patterns, viewpoints, and life rhythms harmonize with his expectation of making it in the streets, casually surviving without providing any useful service to the community.

Where recognizing ladders of service as opportunities and devising methods for ascending from rung to rung on them are cultural imperatives, the whys for doing so are obvious. Where the imperatives are absent, leadership has to devise strategies for manufacturing them. Sincere and dedicated leadership is needed to clear up the chaos and confusion in the J-community. The disorder calls for leaders who understand the problems and who are able to steer youthful energies up healthy avenues. They must have the courage to stand in the teeth of the storm of criticism and ridicule that their initial innovations will evoke until the winds subside and the people are ready to listen to three-dimensional proposals. Good leadership will not come from schoolteachers or administrators bent on being good guys, attempting to become one of the fellows, and trying to rap and quip and relate to youngsters twenty and thirty and forty years their junior who have no interest in study and discipline and structure.

No violence would be done to accuracy if the Jive community were dubbed a pit of babble. Huge sectors of its self-perception relative to mainstream reality need rethinking, refocusing, and rearticulating. As suggested earlier, the term "black power," for example, was never clarified. It came into use in the 1960s, and for years rolled off the tongue of everyone interested in reforming the social contract between the races. Its meaning was left to individual interpretation. Definitions ranged from the sublime to the asinine. At one end of the pendulum, black power simply meant that no eligible Afro-American would be barred from the voting booth anywhere in the country. This implied that black citizens would be proportionately represented in their jurisdiction. It meant that a 30-percent-black city could expect to have three Afro-Americans on a city council of ten members, and that the Negro section of town could expect city services like trash pickups and paved streets—which were often the exception rather than the rule prior to the 1960s. This definition of black power was conceived to mean that a community with a black majority could have a black mayor if it considered a contending black candidate the best qualified to conduct the city's business. In short, "black power" was a positive modernization of the time-honored principle of majority rule, even if the majority were Afro-American.

At the other end of the definition spectrum, C and J believed that "black power" meant the unrestrained ascendency of his definition of proper social conduct. At the peak of black power's exuberance, jaywalking increased exponentially in the center cities. Illegal parking, double parking, and even triple parking became commonplace. C and J no longer let an expletive slip out now and then as they walked the streets. Four-letter words came out loudly, clearly, and repeatedly.

Duplicating the manner in which he invoked "black power" to his detriment, the Jive youth distorts the entire range of edifying community ideas and activities in harmful and self-destructive ways. He invariably strikes discordant notes on crucial issues. When he is not considered a buffoon he is thought to be lazy, ignorant, destructive, or disruptive, to name a few of the disparaging cognomens thrown his way.

An intelligent and concerned leadership would counsel C and J against hanging out. A trip through a center-city neighborhood during the summer between 11:00 A.M. and the following 3:00 A.M. finds rows of front steps full of loiterers. Horsing around and jiving is, in a way, worse than doing nothing, because it reduces the gathering to some least common denominator of ignorance and violence and crime. These urban lotus-eaters are in dire need of channels into which they can constructively direct their considerable energies. They should be offered courses in mechanics, electricity, refrigeration, plumbing, and so on, although they have earlier rejected the disciplines of basic English and arithmetic and writing. Any learning activity would be better for them than squandering their preparatory years, awaiting a new playground and better "afaletic" equipment.

14. The Need for Poise and Control

Any Afro-American spokesman functioning in the three-dimensional common-sense mode would sooner or later feel constrained to discuss poise and emotional control with his constituents. These complementary qualities are conspicuously absent in the personality of the Jive community. The word *cool* is often employed, but cool is itself half jive, and in the Jive community it comes off as such.

Early on, the J-youngster learns the technique of the thoughtless rejoinder to any observation, sensible or nonsensical. His replies are mindless clichés arising out of his culture. The fatuous quip is taken up so early and practiced so consistently that a youngster never acquires the capacity to make thought-out replies to serious questions and observations. The mindless cliché quipped quickly becomes the only method of communication intelligible to his ears. His programmed retort to any suggestion, question, or observation insures that J-youngsters will not recognize an idea with implications outside their own circumscribed experience.

It is at this stage of their lives that the one-way filter screen between them and the outside world is activated. Exogenous input stops for all intents and purposes, and the likelihood of getting a handle on the practical problems of life recedes like the tail of an aberrant meteor. By the time they realize they are in a trap without a manual to understand its mechanisms, the only avenue into which they can direct their energy is emotionalism. And at the slightest provocation blind emotionalism escalates out of control. This affects enough of the J-citizens to become normal behavior for the environment and to be accepted as proper conduct. Under the circumstances, normal mainstream poise and control strike J as indicative of weakness, a refusal to become involved, or simple, cold-blooded unconcern. Frenzy is such an integral part of the culture that a vote against it is considered traitorous if cast from within, or an inability to relate to the community if cast from without. Loose handling of one's time and conduct and budget is thought to symbolize the nonchalance that sets the young and carefree apart from those who have been beaten insensate by life. Irresponsibility and the lack of restraint are seen as the proper marks of youth and dynamism.

When an enclave within a larger community has no mechanism for comparing and adjusting its norms to those of the whole community, it becomes increasingly isolated. If its spiritual and moral values and its regard for social niceties and legal rules deviate too severely from community-wide norms, and if it does not care because it fails to realize that it should, it is on the ski slopes to urban barbarity. The enclave is twice cursed when its skids are greased by ignorant or fawning or opportunistic spokesmen who encourage it to continue "doing its own thing."

Poise is characterized by dignity and balance and striking an appropriate posture for a given occasion. It is a function of emotional control, of knowing what the proper conduct should be, and of having an awareness of one's appearance in the eyes of the community. And the larger the community one considers himself a part of, the more cultivated and cosmopolitan his poise.

Few contemporary Afro-American spokesmen seem inclined to help the J-citizen adjust his sights to focus on the concerns of the larger community. Either the aspiring leader misunderstands the problems of those he proposes to lead, or he considers them hopeless. A depressing third explanation of the spokesman's conduct is that he is satisfied to leave J where he is in order to perpetuate his own "leadership" position, wallowing in whatever honor the title bestows, and using the political clout and the administration of the community planning and education "grants" to his own advantage.

A well-prepared, assertive leadership with no ax to grind except the levitation of the C and J youth could work the schools and youth clubs and playgrounds with the messages the youth need to hear. Such a leadership could compound a prescription containing control and manners and industry and study until the idea gained currency, which any three-dimensional, common-sense message eventually will. A slow, upward spiral would begin for many apparently lost youth— more than the mere one or two in a long while whose "deviant" brain chemistry permits them to pick up outside messages and helps them escape the fate of their surroundings.

At no time should Afro-American spokesmen pass up the opportunity to update the C and J definitions of relevance. They should stress that young people in narrow cultural enclosures with limited experience are unequipped to decide what lessons and ideas are relevant to their welfare in a jet-age world of high technology and sophisticated communications systems.

An ethnic community needs a special brand of leadership. This is especially important in a high-visibility community where many inhabitants have developed the ugly-duckling complex. The complex has nothing to do with actual ugliness, but results from perceptions of being different from a perceived ideal. The difference may be disparaged blatantly or subtly. In either case the results can be disastrous. It decimates one's ability to find one's ladder, for example. And if one is shown one's ladder, the complex renders one unable to mount and climb it. Human sensitivities do not function properly under the stress of sustained community and self-depreciation. Some victims are crushed, others become destructive, and still others become mere caricatures of citizens in pursuit of respectability.

The remedy for the ugly-duckling complex for a minority in the process of forging its own legends, whose traditions and roots are neither clearly in one continent nor another, is not, could not, and should not be the time-honored remedy practiced by races and ethnics with ancient traditions. Such traditions take endless years and layers of historical sifting, selection, and omissions. The process is painstakingly exaggerated à la Beowulf the Brave Prince and Roland the Noble Knight fabrications, for example. And nothing less than the long vistas of time and seasoning give these myths and self-perceptions authenticity. It is in this light that all the "black pride" and "black-is-beautiful" breast-beating of a decade ago was so fragile and ineffective and even comical. If it is true, as some reports indicate, that functional illiteracy has increased since 1965, and that even fewer youngsters are motivated to seize the brass ring of opportunity revolving past them every day, the rhetoric and bombast had negative results.

The cure for the ugly-duckling complex is the pride in personal accomplishment, which leads to an inner assurance of self-worth. Afro-American traditions of heroics and accomplishments have not become robust enough in less than a quarter-century of equal opportunity to buoy up an entire race unaided. The accomplishments of many Afro-Americans over the years notwithstanding, each family and individual is still on its own for tradition-making purposes. Relying on pride through association is an attempt to pass a buck that cannot be passed.

Afro-Americans—and Afro-Europeans, for that matter—who have made contributions to mainstream history are seldom listed by race. They are merely recorded as contributors—and are popularly assumed to be white. So since C and J are not readers, they discount the contributions and exploits of, say, Hannibal, Crispus Attucks, Elijah McCoy, (the real McCoy), and Pedro Nino—to name four of at least a hundred who could be listed here—as events unrelated to their race. And to compound the tragedy, with all the positive and hopeful material to be drawn from, the demagogue-oriented spokesmen never venture beyond slave ships and the cat-o'-nine-tails when they attempt to lift the curtain of black history. They engender depression where they could generate hope.

In addition, there are the popular trends and fads with which the Afro-American spokesmen have permitted, and even encouraged, C and J to divert themselves—diversions that turn out to be only minor setbacks for mainstream practitioners, but which prove disastrous for minorities who have yet to learn about coping with society's complexities. The preoccupation with *me* and the obsession with non-stop entertainment are two examples. Indulging in the search for one's roots and identity through the backwaters of the past or practicing omphaloskepsis (contemplating one's naval) are pursuits for mystics or accomplished scholars or cop-outs with relatives who are able to send them an occasional check in emergencies. The C and J youth fall into none of these categories, however.

There are light-years of difference between the portents of a mainstream scion who decides to open the top button of his tight shirt collar—or even to take off the garment and wander shirtless through the streets—and the disadvantaged youth who decides to hate a shirt and tie before he ever owns such an outfit. When the aforementioned scion wearies of shaking his fist at propriety and shouting into the wind, he has a picture frame of culture and connections and order to re-enter. When the disadvantaged youth discerns that man does not live by the brandished fist alone, he has no such structure to step back into. He has no shirt and tie, and if someone made him a gift of them he would not know how to wear them—having spent years defying the conventions that would have taught him.

By the same token, the right to non-stop "fun" which C and J have been encouraged to claim for themselves is reality turned inside out. The relentless search for entertainment and excitement as one's due outside the context of work and duty is the extrovert's equivalent of the psychotic obsession of searching for one's identity.

Middle-class youngsters imbued with the ladders-of-success idea consider entertainment a reward for diligent work. Fun is not to be indulged in before it is earned, nor is it to interfere with work or with the preparation for a career. Moreover, mainstream youngsters recognize the different species of fun. There are physical and competitive fun, social fun, and spectator fun. In addition, there is the type of activity that is fun and edifying at the same time. Many motivated young people entertain themselves reading books—popular and classical literature, history, geography, and even mathematics and science.

The obsession with fun is especially destructive to J. His community and family life are already equivalent to a three-ring circus for activity. Since he has no cultural stabilizers to guide him through the rapids of distraction that surround him and no leadership beacons for orientation, his chances of getting his bearings in the world of reality are small.

15. Lack of Ambition

The Afro-American spokesmen of the last decade and a half have failed to exhort C and J to project their ambitions beyond their own horizons. Ambition is a touchy word in the Jive community. Aiming high is unpopular. The origin of the contempt for upward aspiration is the Jive mentality's disdain for excellence, and the distrust it has for one of its own attempting to escape the restrictions imposed by the lack of skills and education and culture. Any C- or J-parent will sincerely declare his hope for a better education and life for his child. But if the prerequisites for betterment become a reality, if the child begins speaking proper English and pouring over school books late into the night, he stands alone against suspicions and contemptuous jokes from all quarters, including the parents. The effort to become better is the arch transgression against one's community. And the notion stubbornly persists despite its increasing rejection by thoughtful citizens since education went public in the Colonies in 1633. It is a middle-class creed that one should strive for self-improvement. But in Jivedom, one is more likely to be admonished against forgetting one's origins and to "stop trying to become something" one is not.

J-youth especially need to be encouraged to aim at a star. They have no middle-class cultural expectations or role models. Only a precious few are personally acquainted with, say, an electrical engineer, an airline pilot, or an insurance broker, to name a small sample of the types who keep commerce and science humming. These youngsters do not know what makes these types tick, nor do they have any concept of the degrees of discipline and control that go into the execution of what economics textbooks refer to as the higher types of occupations.

16. Lack of Romanticism

Contemporary Afro-American spokesmen are either unwilling or unable to counsel with the C and J youth about romanticism and the specter of pleasure and beauty and delight that always exist just beyond one's reach. They fail to give C and J a glimpse of the spirituality and vision that drove Icarus, da Vinci, and Wilbur and Orville Wright, until man realized the dream he had dreamed of riding the wind like a condor, since he squatted by his fire in the marshes. The spokesmen are uninterested in introducing the youth to the fantasies and ideals that produced the world's enduring ballads and stories and poetry. They miss the opportunity to explore the anatomy of the kind of dream that caused Jacob to work seven years in the desert sun for Rachel's hand in marriage and agree to seven additional years when the original contract developed a hitch after the first septennial.

Chances are small that the J-community will cast up a Wright or a Brontë or a Jacob, but the Afro-American spokesmen should insist upon something better than the unimaginative and unconscionable consumption of every goody, real or imagined, that one happens upon. They should disabuse the youth of the philosophy that the time is always *now* and control is unnecessary; that everything should be gulped with a greedy intake of air and followed by a vulgar burp. And just because sex is out of the closet and the mystery is gone, it does not follow that love has degenerated to nothing more than an athletic encounter with "kicks" followed by boredom and a need for an additional "high." The tradition of scheming and preening and fantasizing, and awaiting the fruition of material prizes and emotional rewards has always defined man. It has been practiced and symbolized since he painted in berry juice and chiseled on the walls of his cave.

Spiritual development and growth and civilizing humility appear to incubate in the moist twilight contemplation of unfulfilled dreams and desires. But aspirations and dreams are also related to one's culture, and a culture given over to gluttonous appetites does not spawn higher aspirations and dreams and spiritual growth.

17. Lack of High-tech Society Survival Instruction

No Afro-American wearing the spokesman's badge has stepped forward during the last two decades to talk to the C- and J-youngsters about the requirements of respectable survival in a complex technical society. The basic concepts have not changed greatly through the successive stages of civilization, but the techniques have. In fact, the techniques differ so drastically that at first glance the entire array of concepts seems different. All ages and stages have required participants to position themselves in the main current of social thought and action. Maintaining one's position in the current requires concerted effort to avoid drifting downstream. In addition, enough navigational skill must be employed to keep one's efforts focused upstream.

From colonial times until the early part of this century America was basically agrarian. The majority of the population lived on farms and in small towns. Life's cadence was slower, and most of the skills necessary for earning a respectable livelihood were easy to learn. A son could expect to walk through life in his father's footsteps, employing the same philosophies and skills that stood his father in good stead. Respectable survival did not require career planning or long years of exacting study. Serious reading, writing, and reckoning were the concerns of the well-placed citizen, or of curious minds who happened to have book, pencil, and paper at hand, and who could devise a respite from the task of wresting food from a begrudging earth.

Ordinary people's lives revolved around their families, their neighbors, their church, and the trips they made to market as the occasion required. They seldom traveled more than a day's ride from home by horse and buggy, or on rare ocassions, by train—and, much later, by a crude forerunner of today's smooth highway cruisers. Their concerns were as narrow as their acquaintances. News traveled slowly and often by happenstance. Life was primarily non-competitive. The townsman was employed by the factory or mine or railroad, where there were usually shortages of manpower, and a son could be brought on the job as soon as he was old enough to work. The farm family lived in isolation and worked hard to maintain itself. The freeholder did what he could for himself, and the tenant farmer did what he was told to do.

In the early 1940s, three events coalesced to produce an epic change in the relationship of the ordinary citizen to the main current of Western cultural thought: The results of universal education came to fruition; World War II occurred; and the electronic media became universal. The war heightened everyone's interest in the flow of world and national events. The conflict was of such magnitude that no citizen was without involvement. Everyone had a son, a husband, a nephew, a cousin, or, certainly, a neighbor called to the colors. The hostilities raged on three continents and on the oceans and islands in-between. Tracking the events through the omnipresent radio breathed living reality into points and coordinates barely touched in high school geography, and which would have otherwise gone unremembered.

The comings and goings, pronouncements and posturings of kings, presidents, ministers, generals, lawmakers, and important industrialists, and their influence on the tides of war, were dutifully reported. Their global activities were analyzed, kibitzed, and often criticized by an ever competitive and aggressive press bent on guaranteeing the people's "right to know." From monitoring the public lives of the great to scrutinizing their private lives was only a short step. For the first time in human history, individuals who had been as remote as the pharaohs were living in glass houses. Some of them reveled in the exposure, while others were horrified by it. But the ordinary citizen delighted in the new media dispensation.

A number of age-old arcana came into plain view. Ordinary citizens with eyes and attention spans of more than ten minutes began to discern what the most observant of their number had long been aware of—and had often acted upon—to work miracles with their futures: Prominent stations in life were not ordained by celestial fiat; the real difference between the movers and shakers of society and the laity was not transcendental faculties, but definable and quantifiable qualities. While advantages of birth and wealth were weighted variables, they were not decisive. Otherwise one could not account for the likes of Abraham Lincoln and Frederick Douglass or Andrew Carnegie and George W. Carver. The crucial qualities for success were the carefully conceived and comprehensive plans for ascending the rungs of a realistically chosen ladder; and the energy, focus, and purposeful pursuit invested in climbing from rung to rung.

Prior to 1919 most of the world's motive power was furnished by the muscles of man and his beasts of burden. In that year the work performed by mechanical equipment overtook the amount done by muscle power. Today more than 98 percent of the world's work is performed by machinery.

The trend toward mechanization was further accelerated by World War II. The new cultural intimacy and familiarity created by education and the news media between the advantaged and the laity has been increasingly strengthened over the ensuing years by the universality of mechanical appliances. In addition to farm machinery, road graders, land clearing equipment, and finally computer-aided design and the robot factory, automation has touched the most mundane activities of life. With the advent of the vacuum cleaner, the automatic clothes washer and dryer, prepared and packaged foods, fast-food restaurants, and chain stores, the ordinary citizen's life is not drastically different from that of his affluent counterpart, as far as the time required to assemble the necessities is concerned.

Western civilization has now become a single entity of communication and commerce. Isolation is a relic of another age. Virtually every village and hamlet, no matter how remote, is constantly bombarded with broadcast sales pitches and news that has been gathered, edited, packaged, and often sensationalized to the limits of credibility. Anyone who wants a deeper analysis of current events may turn to the abundance of newspapers and magazines available. In addition, there are countless books of expert and not-so-expert opinion on practically every subject imaginable.

There are individuals and groups who choose to pursue backwater objectives, however, and remain outside the principal arenas of activity and thought. When the choice is deliberate, those who make it are happy, or at least content, with watching the world go by from a distance. On the other hand, some are excluded because they are either culturally or temperamentally unequipped to cope with the pace and complexities. They are discontent with their lot; they feel unhappy, resentful, and snubbed. The Jive community is one such group. And it perceives its exclusion to be the fault of the system rather than its own. Its problem is complicated. Unlike those who reject the involvement and whatever benefits accompany it, J wants the rewards, but is either unable or unwilling to pay his membership dues.

The concept of joining or not joining the mainstream is baffling for those not already in the current and not naturally gravitating toward it. Getting into the action is as difficult for the inept and untutored as staying out of an exposure to the news is. The mainstream infrastructure consists of essentially three interlocking systems: mechanization, automation, and communication—all behaving as elements within the Delphian matrix of high finance.

Except for a few highly skilled trades, the present labor market in the developed world is essentially white-collared. Employment which lends itself to respectable survival is of a cognitive nature. It includes such areas of endeavor as experimentation, research, development, monitoring, communications, interpreting, designing, and reporting.

The rapid development of a culture that requires so large a percentage of its population to participate on the cognitive level is revolutionary. It leaves large segments of its citizenry in shock. If humanity's five thousand years of civilization could be distilled into twenty-seven years and injected into a mythical individual, the resulting twenty-seven-year-old would have been introduced to the world of forced abstract thinking only within the last two months of his life—if one reckons the time of pervasive automation from the 1950s. That is, the ratio of five thousand years to thirty years is the same as twenty-seven years is to two months. So the first twenty-six years and ten months of this mythical individual's life would have been spent in an overwhelmingly kinesthetic rather than a cognitive world. And unless he had a definite predilection for abstractions and complexities, a great deal of coaching would be necessary to bring him "up to speed." The problem would be colossal if the individual did not consider himself a part of the community and had no interest in its inner workings, as is the case with J.

Helping the J-youngster to get his bearings and to learn to fend for himself in the cognitive environment is the proper task of the spokesmen who have his ear. Obviously, many of them fail to comprehend the nature and depth of J's disability vis-à-vis mainstream technology and communications. This is easy to understand of spokesmen who are bluffing their way through life as black expert counselors and advocates. Their focus is on all the "wrongs" of society rather than on an understanding of it. On the other hand, it is difficult to believe that some of the more thoughtful spokesmen lack insight into the obvious reasons underlying J's dislocation in the modern world.

During the transition period that began with the brief equipoise between muscle power and motive power and ended with the arrival of automation, J had a breathing spell. There were enough of the dwindling common labor jobs left to accommodate the J-citizens, who numbered less than 10 percent of the population. The untrained laborers who left the rural areas for the cities experienced no need to revise their traditional ways of preparing for employment. But by the late 1950s and early 1960s, their time had run out. And now as their progeny thrash about in anger and confusion, the spokesmen with whom they identify add to the chaos by counseling bellicosity rather than serious career preparation.

The study and preparation concept is frequently expressed by public figures of all persuasions and in a variety of contexts. Unfortunately it is not transmitted through the filter screen surrounding the Jive community. For effect, the message has to be transmitted by the spokesmen who have J's ear.

18. Lack of Appreciation for Current Complexities

The current crop of Afro-American spokesmen has not chosen to counsel J about the anatomy and rewards of appreciation. Consequently the youngster has no affinity for anything that fails to catch the untrained eye or ear at first brush. The idea that the tastes that provide the greatest rewards are acquired ones—usually under tutelage—would strike him as foreign and pretentious. What is more, if anyone in the community begins to toy with such fancy notions as, say, chess or classical music or meteorology, or even serious school work, for that matter, the community quickly—and usually permanently—brings him up short for his aberrant ways. If there is one sentiment with which the entire community is in accord, it is the prohibition against anyone's aspiring to expand his horizons. The opportunity is never missed to hurl the wet blanket, "Ain't the folks and things around here good enough for you?" Thus the capacity to appreciate any quality beyond one's narrow confines is smothered. Consequently, J has never bumped heads with the notion that appreciation requires an acquaintance with the anatomy of the subject considered. Zeno's paradox, for example, remains a paradox without an understanding of a convergent series. Familiarity with the idea of convergence implies at least a reasonable mastery of fractions, decimals, and elementary algebra. But in addition to understanding convergence, the paradox cannot be thoroughly appreciated without some comprehension of the cultural limitations of Roman numerals as compared with the Arabic genre as a computing language.

A better appreciation of an automobile coincides with the comprehension of a four-cycle engine, its cooling and lubrication systems, and its vibration dampers. And one has a greater appreciation of the television as it produces pictures of a dynamic event a continent away if he at least understands the carbon-pile principle behind the early telephone and its relation to the photoelectric cell.

Travel has more meaning to the voyager acquainted with the history and geography of the places the trip touches. In the same way, a chess game is beautiful and exciting to anyone who knows the rules and tactics and defenses and has played enough to recognize some of its subtleties and strategies. One cannot appreciate civilizing pursuits without having engaged in the effort to acquire some knowledge about the qualities that make them civilizing.

A fair index of an individual's inclination for exploring and appreciating the anatomy of an article or event is the type of music he enjoys. The most primitive music is the unaccompanied beat. People are born responsive to a rhythmic thump; they are attuned to it by their mother's heartbeat as embryos. A rhythmic beat can be soothing or exciting, depending upon its volume and accent and intensity. The acquaintance with a muffled cadence precedes breathing and crying and sucking and is more primitive than fear and sex and anger. A baby enjoys a rattle before it is able to balance itself on its hands and knees. It makes its own music banging its plate with its spoon in its highchair.

Just above the beat on the scale of complexity is the chant. The chant may be rendered *a cappella* or accompanied by the beat. Small children chant spontaneously, and primitive societies and modern religions rooted in antiquity observe chanting rituals. The chant may arise instinctively, or it may be employed deliberately because its universal appeal is sure-fire.

Above the chant is melody; and beyond melody, the different complexities of harmony reside. And heavy orchestration forms the perch of structured music. At each step, the compositions require increasing degrees of effort and thought and skill. They appeal to increasingly complex mental, emotional, and aesthetic processes. Thousands of people enjoy the entire range of music, but since study and practice and discipline are the precursors of complex mental and aesthetic capabilities, the more thoroughly developed personality has the greatest affinity for complex music.

19. The Inability to Cope with Abundance and Leisure

The current Afro-American spokesmen are oblivious to what is perhaps J's most pressing problem: his inability to cope with abundance and leisure, and the freedom they bestow. The young spokesmen themselves are unlikely to have had first-hand experience with the mould of scarcity out of which the world's classical economic laws were formulated, and by which most of the people of the world are scourged to this day. Again, this is because the spokesmen are not serious readers of history and are not aware of the economic realities that either deny opportunity or define its dimensions.

Until very recently, most of humanity spent at least six of the seven days of the week waging an unending, and sometimes losing, battle against hunger. From an unthinkably early age, rural children were given little axes or hoes or water buckets and taught to pool their energy with the family effort to keep the lean wolf of starvation away from the door. In the cities, it was into the industrial sweatshops for the children in order that their pitiful earnings could be added to the families' slim coffers. And the mining burgs saw their prepubescent population take up picks and shovels for an introduction to their collier career—and often to a quick death by accident, or one that advanced more slowly by way of ruptures, rheumatism, silicosis, and grotesquely premature bodily deterioration.

Following ten to twelve to sixteen hours of the kind of drudgery required of life preceding the pervasive machine, young people had no time for hanging out and beer busts and drugs. After a few hours of exhausted sleep between shifts, they were literally back in harness. Now that youngsters have been machine-freed from the endless physical and mentally deadening toil, the J-youth have been caught up in the equally deadly trap laid by the possession of an over-abundance of wayward energy. Until the very recent turn of the pages of history, young people who found themselves able to avoid drudgery realized their fortunate circumstances. Reflecting the pre-automation community attitude toward work, they felt compelled to fashion themselves worthy of their good fortune and of the community from which the blessing came. They undertook self-improvement programs through study or enlistment in the armed services or in any other worthy enterprise that presented itself. By contrast, J-community spokesmen have convinced the youngsters that they have a right to live idly, and, moreover, that their idle existence is just as worthy of community respect as that of any productive citizen's.

Compared to historical indices, as well as current world standards, only a relative few people in the United States have less in material resources than an adequate livelihood requires. A properly ordered purchasing list is another matter, however. And this is nowhere more apparent than in J's neighborhood. Any morning finds pre-teenagers sauntering along the sidewalk to school breakfasting on candy bars and carbonated drinks from the corner store. The money could have been better spent for nourishing hot cereal and milk and juice for a sit-down meal at home. People in their early twenties drive the streets in expensive cars, wearing overpriced shoes and designer shirts and jeans. Few of them have ever been in for a dental checkup or have ever had their teeth cleaned. An endless list of such examples could be cited. At the same time, self-appointed spokesmen for the community continue to scream that the community's problems are imposed from the outside. No suggestion is ever made that their shopping lists could be reordered, or that their leisure time could be used for self-improvement and for family and community service.

Chapter 3
THE GOLDEN CENTURY OF AFRO-AMERICAN LEADERSHIP

GREAT LEADERS OF THE PAST

1. Douglass, Washington, and Du Bois

The Golden Century of Afro-American Leadership fell between the early 1840s and the late 1940s. This period was dominated by Frederick Douglass, Booker T. Washington, and W. E. B. Du Bois. A number of other talented individuals moved in and out of the leadership arena during the century, but none cast the long shadows that this trio projected. A number of able men arrived on the scene ahead of the Golden Century trio, and other significant leaders followed, but the large tracks of Douglass, Washington, and Du Bois practically obliterated the ones made earlier and were too large to be filled by those who followed. Their century represented the high-water mark for Afro-American leadership.

The trio had the full measure of basic qualities essential to ethnic helmsmanship. All were excellent advocates, mentors, and spokesmen. In addition, they were forceful, authoritative, and had an abundance of the charisma necessary to attract and hold an enthusiastic following on a national scale. They understood the background and the strengths and weaknesses of their constituencies. And Washington, even more so than the other two, had an uncanny historical presence of mind. His comprehension of what the Afro-American needed, and why he needed it, was complete.

The Golden Century trio generated an energy field that complemented the efforts of leaders with narrower but indispensable talents. The psychodynamics of a suppressed minority population spark easily recognizable needs for a wide variety of endogenous mentors. Individuals who have deciphered the codes of survival and occasional success under extremely adverse circumstances recognize the ineptitude they see in others of less experience and judgment. With few exceptions they are inclined to give chalk talks where they are needed. The local mentors define the nodes in a network that must be energized by leaders of greater prestige. And the scattered themes are of little consequence without the orchestration and authentication of leaders of national stature. During the lives and times of Douglass, Washington, and Du Bois, a center of gravity of national leadership existed. It functioned to weave all the strands of counseling and struggling and protesting that emanated from the Afro-American community into a whole cloth of racial focus and momentum.

2. Speaking on Behalf of, To, and For the Afro-American Community

As a result of the circumstances attending the Negro's history in the United States, most Afro-American leaders arrived on the public scene in the role of advocates. At different times and places, as the occasion required, they were found demanding freedom, clamoring for justice, or exposing immoral, unchristian, and inhuman crimes perpetrated against black people. They were acting *on behalf of* their constituency.

Other leaders donned their togas of office as mentors, speaking *to* the Afro-American community. As one would expect, many of the leaders in this category usually began as schoolteachers. They belonged to that special group driven to impart knowledge and habits and attitudes required of individuals who desire and deserve freedom and opportunity and responsibility.

On occasion there have been persons who made their initial public appearance speaking *for* the Afro-American community—and who later developed into full-scale three-dimensional advocates, mentors, and spokesmen, able to speak *on behalf of, to,* and *for* the community. Those reaching full-scale leadership status who launched their careers as spokesmen *for* the community are rare, however. Speaking *for* a constituency represents the final phase of authoritative leadership. Anyone attempting this phase as a starting point is usually self-appointed or a designee of some dubious special interest. More often than not, the self-appointee is an egomaniacal opportunist. He lacks the discernment to recognize his inability to speak for a group whose confidence he does not have, and he fails to fathom his incompetence to articulate its feelings without an in-depth understanding of its needs and desires.

3. Frederick Douglass's Development

Frederick Douglass began his career speaking *on behalf of* Afro-Americans. At abolitionists' meetings held at the Negro church he attended in New Bedford, Massachusetts, Douglass, as an escaped slave, began quite naturally to rise to his feet during the course of the discussions and to describe firsthand the misery and mistreatment of the slaves in the southern United States.

He was able to describe his own experiences as well as the condition of slaves in general so graphically that he soon gained local fame as a public speaker. Influential people not ordinarily found in attendance at Negro church gatherings began appearing when Douglass was scheduled to speak. By the autumn of 1841, he was invited to become a lecturer for the Massachusetts Anti-Slavery Society. Douglass took the assignment with pleasure. His three sisters, a brother, and many of his friends and acquaintances were still held in slavery. He saw the lecturer's position as a podium of opportunity from which he could speak on behalf of them all.

Douglass's delivery was so attractive and convincing because he was able to articulate with force and energy without being vehement. He was as well received on the national abolitionist circuit as he had been in New Bedford, and his reputation as an orator grew each year. He lectured for the Connecticut, the Rhode Island, and the Massachusetts Anti-Slavery Societies. In addition, he addressed one hundred anti-slavery conventions from New Hampshire to Indiana for the New England Anti-Slavery Society between 1841 and 1845.

After four years on the lecture circuit, Douglass decided to write a book. He felt that he had more to put into the anti-slavery body of thought than the mere recounting of events that occurred in his life as a bondsman. He wanted to level his sights on slavery as an institution and comment on the economic and moral and philosophical aspects of the practice. A number of his fellow abolitionists were aghast at the idea. They would not hear of his reformatting his presentation. They thought that the extremely successful formula that he had developed for himself and the entire abolitionist movement should be left intact, and that by philosophizing on the abstractions of slavery as an institution, Douglass would forfeit the credibility that he had garnered in such good measure through speaking from his personal experience. Finally, his dissuaders drove home a really telling point: They reminded Douglass that his articulate presentation, good English, and perfect bearing caused many people to doubt that he had ever been a slave in the first place. And becoming a philosopher would deliver the *coup d'état* to his authenticity. His greatest worth to the cause, they contended, was the example he portrayed of the kind of intelligence and talent that resided in a people held in bondage. Nothing could be done beyond the role he was presently playing to more thoroughly stamp the institution of slavery as insane as well as criminal.

Douglass heard his dissuaders out, and considered their sincerity and the merits of their case. Then he settled on a compromise. He persisted in writing his book, but decided to make it an account of his life as a slave. With that done, those who doubted that he had been born, bred, and raised to manhood in bondage could read the record for themselves.

The compromise Douglass worked out with his colleagues was an auspicious one. He called his book *Narrative of the Life of Frederick Douglass* and had it published in the summer of 1845. The first edition sold quickly, and Douglass's popularity was further enhanced in the abolitionist circles. One of the prices of his higher visibility, however, was the certainty that sooner or later he would fall into the clutches of bounty hunters. After all, he was still legal property in the state of Maryland. And there were hundreds of human bloodhounds scouring the northern states sniffing out escaped slaves. For handsome rewards and pro-slavery accolades, and by authority of the often-challenged Fugitive Slave Acts of 1793, these ferrets whisked dozens of runaways southward across the Mason-Dixon line every year. In fact, they often kidnapped free Negroes, of whom there were five hundred thousand in the United States in 1849, and sold them into slavery. More often than not, the bondsmen were severely punished, many were re-sold into sterner environments, and some were murdered in ghoulish vengeance.

The recapture of so popular a runaway as Douglass would have been a feather in any bounty hunter's cap and cause for jubilation for the entire pro-slavery Confederacy. So, at this point in his career, Douglass and his brain trust decided he would be well advised to take a trip abroad. He could use the opportunity to speak to English audiences about the evils of slavery. His friends were certain that he would be well received. They imagined that after hearing Douglass's intelligent oratory and seeing his upright bearing, the English would be horrified that such a specimen of manhood had actually been held in slavery only seven years earlier. They would be revolted at the thought that other such individuals were still held in bondage. And who of all Americans but the southern gentry, with their baronial pretensions, would be more deeply cut by English censure?

Douglass's decision to go abroad was as fortunate as his decision to write his book. He traveled through England, Ireland, and Scotland for two years. Wherever he went he spoke before large and sympathetic audiences, and to his everlasting amazement he encountered no racial prejudice of any kind. In 1846 a group of friends he had made, headed by two sisters named Anna and Ellen Richardson of Newcastle, raised funds, purchased his freedom, and presented him with the bill of sale. Except for his full commitment to the anti-slavery movement in the United States, Douglass would have very happily remained in England for the rest of his life.

After more than six years of speaking on behalf of his race, and writing against slavery and for freedom in his book, and nine years after having been held in slavery, Frederick Douglass established his newspaper, the *North Star,* in December 1847. The purpose of the *North Star* was to attack slavery and to promote the intellectual improvement of the Negro. The newspaper lived up to its objectives. In reality it was more influential than Douglass's oratory because it reached a larger audience. It was widely quoted and reprinted in both Europe and America. And unlike the usual ephemeral abolitionist publications of the period, it survived well into the Civil War. In fact, it came within one year of outlasting the war. The paper was re-organized twice. It began as the *North Star,* became *Frederick Douglass' Paper,* and, eventually, *Douglass' Monthly,* but its purpose remained steadfast. It convinced legions of readers of the utter barbarity of holding a race of people in involuntary servitude; of writing them off as childlike and irresponsible when they were obviously capable of producing—against all odds—an orator, thinker, and writer of the caliber of its editor.

4. Douglass Becomes a Full-scale Leader

Individuals with the force of personality and artistic talent to turn others to their opinions and sometimes to tears often have moods that swing from exuberance to depression. They ride the crest of exaltation when pleasing and persuading, and wallow in the trough of melancholia when the tides of enthusiasm and opinion fail to favor their course. Douglass was famous for his ability to electrify audiences from a rostrum. Less was known of his states of depression, which coincided with the frequent financial close shaves of his newspaper business. He was especially aggravated at what he considered the lack of support his publication received from the half-million-strong free Negro community. It was in these moments of depression that he spoke *to* his constituents, pointing out facts he thought they should bear in mind. In the process he became a full-scale, tri-faceted leader, speaking *to,* as well as *on behalf of* his clients. He had long since been a speaker *for* them, explaining what they wanted and felt, and expressing their opinions on important matters.

During his moments of despair Douglass sometimes inserted an occasional admonition into an editorial addressed to his Negro readership. At one point he indicated to the community how thoroughly it confounded him that less than one-half of one percent of them seemed in any way concerned about their brothers and sisters in slavery. No more than fifteen hundred of the half-million were willing to pay for and read an anti-slavery newspaper. He advised that people ought not to remain idle and indifferent about matters that needed improvement.

On at least one occasion Douglass fretted about the shiftless attitude that he had discerned in some of the free Negroes. No power on earth, he fumed, could improve the lot of people unconcerned about their own welfare, nor did the unconcerned deserve blessings for which they were unwilling to work. Douglass also observed that he felt there was a great deal of truth in the assertion that, to some degree, people receive the rewards of which they are worthy. Furthermore, he noted that a community looks up to industry and intelligence and self-respect, and down on sloth. He advised that the black race could not be improved upon and elevated any faster and farther than it was willing to improve and elevate itself; that the race would stand or fall on its own merits.

On still another occasion Douglass observed that, as far as he had been able to ascertain, people who earned a commodity, whether it was freedom or property or whatever, were far better prepared to defend it than those to whom such things were given. He wondered if there was any point in standing a man on his feet if he was just going to fall and bash his head on the pavement once his support was removed. During his admonitory editorials Douglass left no room for excuses. He countered special pleas before they could be offered up. In his opinion, poverty could not be used as a stalking horse for not buying the things one needed when the frivolities one wanted were always on hand. And he was infuriated that he could get no more than fifty attendees at a national "rights" conference when an Odd Fellows convention or a Free Mason conclave regularly drew five thousand brothers. He thought that more time should be spent on noble causes and less on glittering follies; that the black man should not imitate the inferior activities of the majority race and neglect reflecting the superior ones. In an often-made reference to education, Douglass admonished the Negro community to educate its children even if doing so required eating coarser food and having fewer clothes. He thought the sacrifice would pay off farther down the road in a more intelligent and informed group who could better order their lives and cope with their problems.

5. Booker Washington's Development

Booker Washington began his leadership role by speaking *to* his constituency. After graduating from Hampton Institute in Virginia, he returned to his hometown in Malden, West Virginia, and taught school for three years. Teaching was right for Washington. From the first year in the classroom, he threw himself into his work with a missionary zeal. Had the conditions surounding his life remained static, he might have taught in Malden for the remainder of his years—even without pay—for the sheer pleasure of passing on his prescription of the precepts and facts so desperately needed by the pupils he encountered there.

An extremely unlikely set of circumstances must have surrounded each child's presence in Washington's classes in those primeval days of Afro-American education. The students' parents were less than twenty years out of bondage, poor and illiterate, with no experience in budgeting, planning, or even sanitation. They were only beginning to get the hang of fending for themselves. The vast majority of the families were large and needed every member's contribution to their meager sustenance. The notion had been drilled into their heads that education ruined a youngster; that it rendered him "uppity" and disdainful of work. And most were inclined to the view that parents should get what tariff they could out of their children before the children grew up and started families of their own.

It took a real witch's brew of ambition, imagination, recklessness, and hope to permit children to spend hours sitting at a desk, pouring over alphabetics and numerics, when they could have been gainfully wielding hammers or shovels, or axes. That first generation of literacy seekers brought little more to Washington's classes than faith in things unseen.

He instructed them in the use of the reader, the speller, the arithmetic book, and much more. He was equally insistent that they become skilled with the washcloth, the comb, and the toothbrush. To many of his students, Washington was the first to introduce these grooming paraphernalia.

During the course of his own education, Washington had perceived that the preparation for progress entailed training the whole person—mentally, physically, and morally. According to his lights, a trained mind and a clean body were consubstantial. He also considered good conduct, an organized schedule, and promptness to be component parts of an educated individual. He was determined to pass these values on to his charges, and no detail that he considered tributary to this personality profile was too small for his attention.

6. Early Recognition of Washington's Talent

By the time Washington arrived in Tuskegee in 1881 at the age of twenty-five, he had accumulated considerable administrative and public relations experience. He was head of Hampton's night school when General Armstrong, the Institute's principal, received an inquiry from the Tuskegee Commission. The Commission wanted the general to recommend a principal for the new institute which it planned to establish.

The commissioners had a white man in mind, of course. No Negro had ever headed an institution of learning at that time. And just sixteen years removed from slavery, the thought of a Negro heading an organization of any consequence never crossed anyone's mind. But General Armstrong had been so favorably impressed with Washington's conduct of the night school, however, that he recommended the young man for Tuskegee. And he did so with such enthusiasm that the commissioners offered Washington the position.

General Armstrong had invited Washington to deliver the commencement address at Hampton two years earlier. The invitation was a signal honor. How often does a graduate of only four years give the commencement address at his alma mater? The honor is usually bestowed upon a prominent scholar, an administrator, or, in the case of a private school like Hampton—always in need of funds—upon some industrial or religious grandee whose organization might be disposed to making a substantial financial contribution.

Washington's address obviously verified the good impression made during his tenure as a student there. And, in addition, another occurrence had transpired to score points in his favor. He had sent four of his Malden graduates to Hampton, and they had placed well enough on the entrance examination to be put into advanced classes. Either all Malden students were very bright or Washington was an excellent and thorough teacher. Soon after he resumed his West Virginia classroom duties, he received the offer to head the Hampton Indian School.

In 1878, a year prior to his commencement address at Hampton Institute, Washington's oratorical promise had been recognized by the Committee to Relocate the Capital of West Virginia. The twenty-two-year-old schoolmaster had been asked by the Committee to stump the state on behalf of having the capital moved to Charleston. At the time the capital was unsatisfactorily located in the far northern panhandle of the state at Wheeling. Wheeling was nearer to Pittsburgh and Akron—the two cities to which it was an apex of a natural trade triangle—than it was to the geographical or temperamental center of West Virginia. Three cities, including Charleston, were in the process of competing for the prize.

Washington derived tremendous enjoyment from representing the Charleston Committee. He was well received wherever he stopped, and he was sufficiently impressive to have a number of people suggest that he begin reading law and go into politics. He thought the matter over, and believed that he could be a successful politician. But characteristic of the way he perceived his teaching mission at that early age and forever afterward, he felt it unthinkably selfish to seek personal success to the abandonment of the vast majority of his people to abject ignorance, a condition he was just beginning to help alleviate. So after finishing his Charleston Committee work he returned to his teaching duties at Malden. And there he would have remained had he not been called away to a greater opportunity for service.

7. Washington, the Resourceful Schoolboy

Once at Tuskegee, Washington found the institute to be only an idea—a $2,000 appropriation for teachers' salaries, and two shacks that were hardly more than chicken coops. He realized that his work was cut out for him if he ever hoped to have Tuskegee approach Hampton in any sense of the word.

One of three routes would have been open to anyone less resourceful than Washington: He could have thrown up his hands, quit the scene, and returned to Hampton where there was already adequate equipment and a viable program within whose context a great deal of opportunity for service existed; he could have resigned himself to make do and struggled hopelessly on against the odds until his ambition and physical strength burned to cinders; or he could have staged a confrontation with the Commission and blown the whole idea to bits. But Washington was resourceful. He had been born a slave in what is now a suburb of Roanoke, Virginia, and had begun working in a West Virginia coal mine at the age of nine, soon after the Civil War. A few years later he had persuaded a reluctant stepfather to let him work a split shift. He may have been the inventor of the work-study program. Working from four to nine o'clock in the morning, stopping to attend school, then returning to the mine for two additional hours of work after grappling with the three r's was the way he began his education. And at the age of sixteen he had walked much of the five hundred desolate country miles between Malden and Hampton, Virginia, to *ask* if he could work for his room, board, and tuition to continue his education.

8. Washington's Discovery in the Woods Surrounding Tuskegee

While he turned the Tuskegee predicament that he had inherited over in his mind, Washington entered into one of his periods of quietude. He considered his next step, awaiting the opportunity that the truly resolute believe coexists with every crisis and is always around the next turn in the road. Not one to squander time, he fell into the habit of taking long walks through the countryside surrounding the village. He wanted to get a feeling for the locale and the nature of the homes and families of the youngsters with whom he would have to deal.

As accustomed as he was to seeing poverty and disorganization, he was appalled at the living conditions of the former slaves. Many of them lived in ramshackle cabins with only a single family bedroom, in conditions so crowded that modesty and morality were out of the question. With a minimum of ingenuity and a hammer and saw, they could have gotten building materials from the woods surrounding them and made any home repairs and additions necessary.

It was equally incredible to Washington that the black people living in the fields and woods around Tuskegee ate as they did. The black-belt soil was some of the richest in the world. Figuratively speaking, a seed thrown on the ground would spring up quickly enough to strike the hand of the sower. Yet the inhabitants were subsisting on a year-round diet of corn bread and salt pork. Their problems were not shiftlessness, but pathetic ignorance. They all grew cotton right up to their cabin doors, with every member of the family working in the fields from sunup to sundown. But the solution to their most elemental problem had simply never occurred to them, nor had anyone ever caucused with them about it. With a modicum of ingenuity and effort they could have spread their tables with vegetables and poultry in abundance—avoiding the multiplicity of physical and mental malnutritive maladies that plagued them.

9. Washington Launches his Building Program

Within a year or two after Washington put his hand to the task in Tuskegee, he learned of a large farm for sale a few miles out in the countryside. A quick inspection revealed that the land would be the ideal spot to start building the kind of physical plant he had in mind.

With his characteristic drive, tempered by enough diplomatic circumspection to avoid upsetting the Tuskegee Commission or the Alabama Legislature, Washington set about acquiring the financing for his venture. He turned first to his mentor, General Armstrong. Between them they worked out a plan, one detail of which included a personal loan from the general to cover a part of the cost.

Once the enterprise was underway, with the use of the farmhouse and the few surrounding buildings as classrooms, dormitories, and a chapel, the school began to acquire the features that would make it unique. With his own sleeves rolled up, Washington set aside certain periods of the day to lead the male students in manual labor. As he saw the matter, there was land to clear, vegetable gardens to cultivate, and fruit trees to set out. Selling his students on manual labor and industrial education was no easy task. Their notions of education were predicated on the avoidance of labor. They had arrived at Tuskegee nursing visions of themselves spending the remainder of their lives reading and discussing Latin, Greek, and other arcane lexicons in the way their parents had imagined refined white folk did. When the word began circulating abroad that the Tuskegee curriculum contained manual labor, many of the students arrived with messages from their elders. They insisted that their children were sent to the institute for "book learning." The youngsters could have learned to work with their hands back home on the farm, they contended.

Washington stuck by his guns, however. He maintained that the flurry of activity around agricultural pursuits did not mean that Tuskegee Institute deemphasized book learning. Instead, it signaled the introduction of a process of training the mind on the theoretical and practical levels simultaneously and developing the hands to address what the mind perceives; of developing both the intellectual and kinesthetic feel for one's work akin to the way the surgeon or test pilot does.

The minimum age of admittance to the institute was sixteen years, and the prerequisite was the ability to read and write—a stiff requirement to impose, as it was less than twenty years after it had been illegal to teach a Negro to read. And as in the case of any school for the disadvantaged, the perennial question arose: Should the entrance requirements be lowered so that no one who wanted an education would be turned away? But the policy makers at Hampton and Tuskegee correctly assessed that an institution or organization loses its mystique if any passerby who walks in on a whim is accorded full membership. An applicant should demonstrate his desire to enter by a willingness to exert himself rather than expect an acceptance to be handed to him on a platter.

The beginning academic subjects consisted of arithmetic, reading, grammar, spelling, geography, and natural history. Washington demanded punctuality, and he brooked no excuses for the lack of cleanliness and neatness. He pointed out missing buttons and soiled spots on clothing, and he was practically manic about the use of the toothbrush. And he wanted to infuse the sense of mission he felt toward teaching the disadvantaged into the students who came to Tuskegee.

10. The Spirit of Tuskegee

With Tuskegee Institute developing in Washington's image, the young enrollees from the surrounding countryside discovered that they had opted for a Spartan life. Drinking, smoking, cursing, and playing cards or dice were strictly forbidden. Each hour from the 5:30 A.M. reveille bell to taps at 9:30 P.M. had to be put to good use. The school was organized on a quasi-military basis, just as Hampton had been under General Armstrong. Meals were formal affairs in matters of dress, etiquette, and punctuality. Religious services were held on Sundays. Chapel services and lectures on morals, etiquette, and study were given on designated evenings during the week. Attendance was compulsory. Washington himself spoke to the students at least once per week when he was on campus.

Having come from an environment of poor and illiterate former slaves who had gravitated to jobs in the coal mines, and having seen how their counterparts around Tuskegee lived, the responsibility to improve the lot of the next generation weighed heavily on Washington's shoulders. No one understood the anatomy of their predicament better than he. No one was more aware of the yawning chasm between their origins and what they could eventually become by having enrolled at Tuskegee. And no one was more hopeful and enthusiastic about educating the youngsters and inspiring them with his own sense of urgency to go out into the southland and lift other black folk to a plane of education, training, or viability according to their ability and disposition.

Washington disdained the priestcraft approach to education. He avoided the mumbo jumbo and incantations that inspired awe and fear but little comprehension. He spoke to the students in clear, informal, and easy-to-understand language. He was the mentor extraordinary. He recognized that most people are capable of more than they ever accomplish because the spark of desire and ambition is never ignited in their minds; and on the rare occasions when the spark flares, the self-discipline to kindle it is absent. He believed that ordinary individuals could accomplish beyond themselves if turned in a creative direction, provided with a bit of hand-holding through the first stumbling steps of an effort, and encouraged at crucial steps along the route.

Washington also knew that pedagogy is most effective when the student is attentive and has the learner's attitude—which in less egalitarian days was called humility. Thus his emphasis on discipline and morality. He believed that prior to negotiating the path between hopeless, listless poverty and robust viability, the former slave had to abandon the slave's mentality toward work and assume the journeyman's attitude. A slave hates his work because it is done for the profit and pleasure of someone else. The former slave would also have to abandon the slave's attitude toward property and assume the owner's outlook. He had cared nothing for property because it would never be used for his benefit nor the benefit of his progeny. He only worked to avoid punishment, and through omission, commission, or both, regularly damaged and destroyed animals and implements. And after long years, the ingrained hatred of work and property had become a reflex. The slave's idea of heaven-on-earth was the state of doing absolutely nothing. One of the favorite songs alluding to "Beulah Land" contained a line, "I'm gonna set right down when I get home." Only the most forward-looking of the newly freed men could discern benefits for themselves in work, and in acquiring and caring for property.

Washington did not have to hold seminars, conduct surveys and interviews, and sift through tons of data to understand the mental states, the psychological blocks and disabilities, and the nature of the help his people needed. He had walked through the valley where they were before reaching his position on higher ground. He was acquainted with the factors of life there, including the illiteracy, superstition, despair, groans, grime, and odors, and he knew the route to betterment because he had taken it. He left no stone unturned in his effort to inspire Negro education, skilled tradesmanship, and ownership. He preferred excellence in English for the utility it provided in writing and communication to excellence in Latin and Greek for the appearance of erudition. And because he believed Afro-American advancement to be predicated on the economic rather than the political plane, he was unabashedly committed to the study of agriculture and the building trades.

11. Promises of Assistance and Rumbles of Jealousy

In time, Washington's sincerity and the unassailable common sense concerning what he intended to accomplish at Tuskegee became clear during his speeches. The reasons the accomplishments were needed, and the national benefits that they portended, began to impress the most important industrialists and political operatives of the late nineteenth and early twentieth centuries. Slowly at first, and then with increasing enthusiasm, they began to donate funds to this southern Afro-American educator who talked to them in the kind of hardheaded, no-nonsense language that they understood, used themselves, and believed in.

But at the same time that Washington was tuning in on the wavelength of the can-do captains of industry and the politicians who piloted the ship of state at the time of the country's maximum rate of growth, he was getting into trouble with the radical intellectuals of his own race. They saw him surfacing in too favorable a light with the people who sat at the country's power levers. At the root of the critics' malaise was the ancestral suspicion of the suppressed. They considered sanctions by the suppressor of any move at all by one of their own to be a sure harbinger of additional scourges to come. Nothing in their experience or radical repertoires sensitized them to the possibility of the tack that Washington had taken. The image of an honest broker, thoughtful and persuasive enough to present a case for the relief of suppression based on an enlightened self-interest for all concerned, was beyond their imagination. So it was during that era that the "get Washington" tradition was launched.

Pseudo-intellectuals and kibitzers who make no claim to intellectualism, standing safely back from the downdrafts of the civil rights storms, have taken Washington's statements out of their literal and chronological context down through the decades. They find him guilty of selling out rights that Negroes had never had, or had never dreamed of getting, when Washington was working his magic in the black belt.

12. Washington's 1895 Decision

In 1894, Washington was asked to join the Georgia delegation orga-nized to petition the United States Congress to aid the Cotton States International Exposition planned for Atlanta the following year. And, just as he had consented to join the committee that had succeeded in having the West Virginia state capital moved from Wheeling to

Charleston years earlier, Washington joined the Cotton Exposition Committee.

After the Committee acquired the blessings and aid of Congress, and the planning of the Exposition program was underway, Washington was asked to be one of the speakers. The invitation came as a shock to him—with all the unpleasant connotations that the word "shock" implies. At that point in the history of the United States, and certainly in the adamantly segregationist South, a Negro was not supposed to have any interests beyond scratching out a bare living for himself and his brood. He was not even supposed to contemplate civic or political matters. To be asked to represent a major industrial sector with a speech before an international audience was unheard of. Washington felt trapped. What could he be expected to talk about? It was not likely that the program committee wanted him to sketch a scenario of the trials and tribulations attendant to Negro education. And as far as he had been able to ascertain, the Confederate Establishment's attitude toward the education of its designated hewers of wood, drawers of water, and pickers of cotton did not indicate they had in mind a pitch for aid to education from him.

Before he finally made his decision, Washington wavered between the opposing dilemmas of declining and accepting the invitation. Declining presented the lesser risk. Any mistake associated with pleading off would be one of omission. Tuskegee's financial benefactors and other friends of Negro education from the North would feel that he had shirked an opportunity to outline his usual clear-headed case for Afro-American education before one of the widest audiences to be assembled in the cradle of the Confederacy in a generation. His students and associates, the majority of whom considered him the prototype builder, counselor, and scholar, would be dismayed if he steered clear of the opportunity to advance their mutual cause at whose head he stood by common acclaim. Moreover, he could never be at peace with his own conscience if he failed to make every effort to enlist the aid and goodwill of the South's finest.

He also knew that as dire as the consequences of declining the invitation would be, they would be nothing compared to getting on the stage in Atlanta committing some unforgivable *lapsus linguae.* A mistake would bring down the ire of the Southern Establishment and destroy that sliver of civility and indulgence which alone had stayed the hand and fire torch of the more boisterous elements of the region. The depressed poor whites had looked with jaundiced eyes over the years at the dressed-up Negroes with their heads held high, hurrying business-like along the legs of the scalene triangle connecting the depot at Cheehaw with Tuskegee and the institute on the town's far outskirts.

But the risk notwithstanding, Washington was the same individual who at sixteen years of age had ridden stage coaches, walked, begged rides, and slept under bridges as he made his way five hundred miles over the Blue Ridge Mountains and through desolate countrysides, towns, and woods between Malden and Hampton. He took a careful look and leaped. He wanted to offer a constructive program in the spirit of friendship and regional progress. And he decided to be frank and honest; to move forward with the sale of his concept of Negro education, which he was convinced was a good one.

13. The Substance of Washington's Atlanta Speech

On the appointed day in 1895, Washington stood as tall and straight as an honor guard Marine before the audience at the Cotton States International Exposition in Atlanta and delivered his speech in a measured cadence. In keeping with habits developed as a teacher, he avoided the flowery oratory that was the style of the period and strove to articulate his ideas in words and sentences designed for clarity. His message outlined a practical program for the recently freed Negro, a program constructed in the hope of forging good race relations in the climate that existed in the southern United States at the close of the nineteenth century.

His speeches were effective because they reflected his true convictions. They also reflected his excellent judgment, goodwill, and unshakable faith in the self-help premise. His Exposition speech was no exception.

Washington believed in systematic procedures and ordered priorities; in putting first things first. He believed that the recently freed slaves should stay away from politics. In his opinion, a people just out of bondage had more immediate things to think of than tampering with the machinery of government. Government was something people turned to after having mastered the processes of feeding, clothing, and housing themselves, and the art of maintaining, raising, and training a family. He considered voting a by-product of having become a substantial citizen.

It made no sense to Washington to have legions of unschooled and propertyless individuals, recently out of bondage, exerting political pressure on a system they did not understand; depending upon someone else to interpret its facts and intricacies for them. He also believed that the southern Negro, circa 1895, could best spend his time on basic education and training. He thought that economic viability should have been their first concern, that people just starting up in a competitive, on-going society might not be able to juggle too many balls at once. Under the circumstances they certainly did not need the distractions of politics. It was an indulgence in which they were not ready to engage. Later on down the road, when the Negro was literate, owned property, had his children in school, and had developed meaningful associations with the commercial and agricultural affairs of the community, his connections would naturally draw him into the local, and even national, political process.

Washington thought his prescription represented the natural approach—like planting in spring, cultivating in summer, and harvesting in autumn. He did not think one could force a natural process that would come to fruition of itself in due time and under the proper conditions.

Besides, Washington recognized that the political process in the United States was at a crossroads. The North viewed the body politic from an industrial viewpoint, and the South was in the throes of transition from a bourbon to a bourgeois mentality. He knew that as far as the southern Negro was concerned, the approach to politics was over precipitous terrain around which lethal turbulences swirled, and he thought Negroes should vector into political affairs from a trade, education, and economic landmark. Moreover, the Civil War was barely thirty years past, and the memory of the moral, economic, and political problems that precipitated it were still sore points of Dixie pride and honor. It would ill serve a minority living among the vanquished to make the mistake of siding with the victors. Taunting a lion from outside his cage is one thing, but doing so from within is asking for a mauling.

Consequently, as soon as Washington had made his introductory remarks, he expressed his belief that it was a reflection of his race's inexperience that their first acts of freedom had been stump-speaking and participation in political conventions. With their preparation they would have better served their interests by turning to dairy farming and truck gardening than to seeking seats in Congress and the state legislatures.

Washington did not believe that motion for the sake of motion was a measure of progress. Motion translated into action only when subjected to measure and control and aimed in the proper direction. He was convinced that the Negro should remain in the South. There he was at home and accustomed to the mannerisms and the tempo of life, to the weather, and the folkways. He would be able to learn and practice the trades he needed to make his life viable and acquire the respect of his society.

The Southland was as rich in resources as any industrious soul needed. And the region was expanding agriculturally and industrially by leaps and bounds. Besides, the Negro's skills and labor were needed there. So why go traipsing off in search of one's fortune when one only needed to lower his "bucket" where he was and dip into the sea of wealth and opportunity already surrounding him?

Thus, after Washington expressed his opinion about the Negro and Confederate politics, he admonished the Afro-American to remain in the South. There, he said, "the Negro is given a man's chance in the commercial world" and should be able to "live by the productions of our hands. . . ."

Washington's concept of an in-depth understanding of the industrial and agricultural arts went beyond their manual aspects. According to his lights, building included a knowledge of design, structure, foundation, heating, and drainage. Skillful farming presupposed a knowledge of animal husbandry, soil management, crop rotation, seed improvement, agricultural economics, and related subjects. And, of course, operating a business, including a farm, dairy, or market of any kind, required an understanding of bookkeeping and merchandising, not to mention business ethics and customer relations. An acquaintance with these various disciplines could be summed up in one word: education.

Washington plugged for education at every opportunity. He equated Negro education directly with defense, security, the absence of crime, business and industrial prosperity, political advancement, and, by implication, with a number of additional deep community and moral concerns.

Finally, he assured the audience that discerning Afro-Americans understood that, at the time, it was more important to prepare themselves for the exercise of their legal privileges than to actually exercise them.

And it goes without saying that he renounced social integration and embraced full industrial employment opportunity.

14. The Nation's Gratitude to Washington

Washington's speech struck the right chord. The unassailable common-sense approach to the needs, purposes, and benefits of Negro education for the 1890s that he had articulated so successfully across the northern states—with a few skillful embellishments and blandishments added—was received at least as enthusiastically in the South. Now he had both the North and the South in his corner.

Washington was quoted in newspapers across the country. His popularity skyrocketed. Here was an Afro-American spokesman, speaking in a voice without rancor, hate, or snarls, sometimes even humorously, with a plan for progress for his people that no sane soul could quarrel with. At long last the nation saw in Washington's blueprint and the controlled manner in which he set it forth, the opportunity to heal its wounds and expunge its guilt.

The country had been torn by factionalism, apologia, and guilt concerning the question of Negro bondage since its inception. Before the states united, Quakers and other religious groups had both denounced and renounced slavery. The institution had risen its ugly head, only to be dealt with tentatively, over the drawing board of the Constitution. During the 120 years between 1776 and 1896, such figures as Prince Hall, Richard Allen, Frederick Douglass, Harriet Stowe, Thaddeus Stevens, and Charles Sumner had lambasted the very idea of slavery. And as the nation became more prosperous and civil—one usually accompanies the other—and had more time to behold itself in the mirror, the racial question increased the malaise that was a spot on the halo it had always worn on its self-image.

If Washington could put the thorny race question on the right track, if he could handle it so that everyone concerned could benefit, and if he could keep the Negro question from remaining a source of irritation between the North and the South, as it had been for so long, then he deserved all the cooperation a grateful nation could give him.

15. The Magnitude of Washington's Popularity

The magnitude of Washington's prestige in the 1890s is difficult to grasp in the 1980s. The criteria for measuring intangibles have changed drastically since the advent of universal literacy and the widespread dissemination of newspapers, books, and magazines. In 1890, for example, a "big man" in a town in one corner of a state could be unknown in another corner. Most of his contemporaries could live out their lives without ever hearing of him. The ordinary citizen of that time was born, lived, and died within the circumference of a few miles. Similarly, the travel time between Atlanta and Washington, D.C., in 1890 was greater than that between Atlanta and Cairo, Egypt, in the 1980s. And the goings-on in Washington were more remote and exotic to the citizen who lived in the countryside surrounding Atlanta then than the activities in Cairo and Bahrain are to the equivalent suburbanite now.

The fact that Booker T. Washington had business that took him from Tuskegee to Washington, New York, Chicago, Pittsburgh, Boston, and other important centers a half-dozen or more times per year invested him with the kind of aura which now surrounds international crime fighters and financial operatives who jet back and forth across the world to hush-hush meetings with other important operatives. Add to the enchantment customarily associated with the personality oscillating between important landmarks of influence, finance, and power the overt approval of the national opinion-makers who believed that Washington had found the solution to the most vexing and abiding of the country's problems, and one begins to sense the measure of the esteem in which Washington was held. His stature was all the more significant because of the time of its ascent. The Emancipation Proclamation was only thirty years old. The Confederacy was only beginning to regain its footing. More than 90 percent of the southern Afro-Americans were illiterate, poverty stricken, and still believed that the earth was four-cornered and flat.

In 1896 the *Washington Post* suggested to incoming President McKinley that he appoint Washington Secretary of Agriculture. The department may not have been more powerful then than now— considering its current involvement with agribusiness, finance, research, grants, and allotments—but it touched the lives of more people directly. The vast majority of the citizens of the country were farmers. They did not have the research and lobbying support enjoyed by the agricultural giants of today. But they were more dependent upon departmental advice, directives, and answers to inquiries than the majority of today's citizens.

16. Reaction to Washington's White House Invitation

The leading industrialists of the day made pilgrimages to Tuskegee to visit the Institute. To a man they came away impressed and, in nearly every case, committed to the school's financial aid.

At one time Andrew Carnegie gave $600,000 in United States Steel bonds to Tuskegee. Some hint of the magnitude of the gift may be measured by comparing the price of a quart of milk in the 1890s to its price in the early 1980s. By this standard the gift would amount to approximately $6,000,000 today. A modest 12 percent interest earned on such a handsome sum would be enough to defray the annual expenses of more than a hundred students at Stanford University, leaving the principal intact.

It was at this stage in Washington's career that the world-famous historian, H. G. Wells, invited the Tuskegean to be his house guest in England. And a short time after his inauguration, President Theodore Roosevelt invited Washington to dinner at the White House.

After some reticent feinting and second-guessing, and some rearranging of schedules, Washington accepted the invitation. His national popularity crested at that point. Cresting does not mean crashing, however, and Washington did not lose his stature. He remained by far the most influential Afro-American in the country. But the unwarranted social implications manufactured around the invitation and its acceptance were used to launch repeated attacks against him.

The first salvo came from the southern press. To a newspaper, they were livid. Their hero of a few days earlier had now become an object of scorn. The image of Washington as a latter-day Moses leading his people to some distant, approved "Promised Land" was one thing. The specter of him in a social setting where only the best and luckiest of them would ever hope to sit was quite another matter. The Confederacy made no bones about the fact that it was the social implications of the White House dinner that enraged them. How could they expect the recent bondsmen to accept their inferior status for very long with their leader wining and dining at the pinnacle of society? More than one paper averred that after Washington's visit, no self-respecting southern white woman could ever accept a social invitation from Roosevelt at the White House.

Derogatory songs and poems were written about the event for years afterward. When this writer was a small child there were no radios and television sets, in middle Appalachia at any rate, and parents still told their children stories and sang them songs. His father told him about Chickie Little and the falling sky, and about Little Red Riding Hood. His mother sang little ditties for him and his brother. One of the songs was:

> Booker T. Washington, a big black man,
> To the White House he went one day.
> He went to see the President,
> In a quiet and social way.
> Teddy met him at the door,
> Booker started to grin.
> He would 'ave changed his color,
> But Teddy said, "Walk in,
> We'll have some dinner in a little while,
> (words unremembered) on toast, chicken and veal roast.

It has been more than fifty years since the writer last heard these words. He does not know where his mother learned the song. He never asked. As a pre-schooler he simply enjoyed the tune and the imagery. He missed whatever there was about it that was supposed to be derisive, and if his mother knew, she never said so—nor would she have. By her lights, a four-year-old was not far enough down life's road for an introduction to gloomy sociology.

17. The End of the Racist Recess

Washington was baffled at the South's medieval fury over his White House dinner. He thought he knew the South quite well and had expected to take a few torpedoes from various quadrants. But he did not expect the sustained wrath from the entire southern wing of the Fourth Estate. After all, feasting with the fabulous was not new to Washington. He had dined with President McKinley at the Peace Jubilee in Chicago three years earlier and with Benjamin Harrison in Paris. At one time he had had tea with Queen Victoria.

Washington's observations had led him to conclude that people who managed substantial enterprises were perceptive enough to make elementary distinctions. Obviously it had been clear to McKinley and Harrison and to Queen Victoria that having a repast with Washington was not exactly the same as extending an invitation to any field hand, any more than seeking Leland Stanford's opinion on a transportation problem resembled asking the same question of a spike hand. Yet the august publishing moguls of Dixie, later joined in full cry by the politicians, complained long and bitterly that Booker Washington's presence at the White House within a social context signaled the breaking of the dam of segregation. Great pains were taken to emphasize the similarity between the character, motives, and intellectual endowments of a Washington and those of any ordinary cotton picker.

Thus did the recently deactivated slave-owning mentality reassume its high profile. The professed Christian's primary justification for owning and exploiting another human was his self-conviction that the individual in bondage belonged to a sub-species. The condition had to apply to all individuals of the class so designated, and no matter how exceptional anyone or even any number of them appeared to be, it was characterized as an illusion: a trick with smoke and mirrors.

Since the initial requirement for getting into line for the blessings of liberty and justice was a certificate of membership in the human race, the southern press made a concerted blast against recognizing the former bondsmen as humans.

The black inferiority myth was kept alive for decades, just as the romanticism of bourbon worship was nourished endlessly. Not until Lyndon Johnson—who in time will join Washington, Lincoln, and Franklin Roosevelt in the gallery of great presidents—took the plunge from regional to national politics did the myth begin to recede. Nor, for that matter, did equal opportunity for southern politicians become a reality. Except for Johnson's initiative the national climate would not have been conducive to a Jimmy Carter presidential candidacy, nor to the austral drift of research and industry that heralded the South's metamorphosis from Cotton Belt to Sunbelt.

18. Washington's Antagonists Close Ranks

Once the solid phalanx of Washington's national support broke, his Afro-American adversaries bared their teeth more overtly and tightened their circle of attack around him. An individual who enjoys national acclaim based upon a social philosophy—as Washington did before he had "dinner with Teddy"—draws enemies like a magnet draws iron filings. And the greater the acclaim, the more intense and dedicated to his destruction are his enemies: some out of honest and profound disagreement and others out of malevolence.

Afro-American power struggles have a vicious tradition. The territory for their exercise has been restricted and the landscape, desolate. The only avenues open to professionals until well into the second half of the twentieth century were teaching, medicine, and law. Of these, teaching had the highest profile. As a result it eclipsed the other two. True, the lawyer and the physician were recipients of longer and more exacting training and were required, in addition, to pass strict and comprehensive examinations prior to plying their trades. But they worked in staid, unventilated offices which smelled either medicinal or moldy with books, while the teacher worked out in the community spotlight.

The medical doctor worked with anatomical and skeletal structure, hypertension, pulmonary problems, and their pathologies and restorations. The lawyer's concern was with sifting and refining legal cases and codes, sometimes threaded back thousands of generations to Hammurabi. Both professions were as remote as the planet Pluto from the simple souls, many of whom believed in cure by conjuration, and justice through prayer and supplication.

Concepts that are little understood are even less appreciated in a community of plain folk only a generation or two out of bondage, as most of the Afro-Americans were at the dawn of the twentieth century. More faith was put in the laying on of hands than in consulting a physician, and more store was laid by having the judge's cook speak to her boss than by seeking legal counsel.

The teacher's work, however, bore fruit in the public square. In the community grammar school she held forth with the mysterious laws of arithmetic, grammar, and the arcane technique of penmanship. She changed the life of everyone who came under her influence. In a demonstrable way she transformed the illiterate soul into a literate one. And if the teacher happened to be a male, he was honored with the title "professor."

The star status had its pitfalls, however. Envious individuals in the community maintained a relentless search for cracks in the teacher's armor. The doctor or the lawyer was indulged now and then in a little mischief, but the teacher, never. The teacher was not permitted the usually accepted human foibles in morals or professional demeanor. Morally, she was held to the standards of Caesar's wife and, professionally, was expected to be the intellectual resource of last resort.

Washington embodied all the magic and hegemony of the rural professor plus an additional national dimension. He had enemies located in many of the important Afro-American population centers throughout the country who nursed envies and jealousies of a national scope. Some of his detractors were thoughtful and scholarly; some were hotheads. Some thought Washington was employing questionable methods in his effort to improve the Negro's lot, and others were convinced that his philosophy was unquestionably detrimental in the long run.

The dissenters in Boston and Washington, D.C., had no doubt that Washington's compromise on voting rights in lieu of an opportunity to study agriculture and a few obsolescent trades, with the hope of coming into full citizenship through the economic back door, was a grievous mistake. They thought it meant losing forever the opportunity to take a manly stand in the teeth of a storm of hate and intimidation to demand what was a self-respecting citizen's just due.

19. Washington Stays his Course

Throughout the years in which Washington's adversaries rained scorn and criticism on his head, he continued quietly and effectively with his work. From all outward appearances he paid little or no attention even to Du Bois's disapproval. The Tuskegean remained calm, controlled, and productive all his life. He defended his views on industrial education by pointing out the emphasis that Germany, the seat of intellectualism at the time, placed on the mechanical arts.

In addition to sticking to his game plan concerning the needs of the black masses, Washington exerted a great deal of effort on the civil rights front. He did everything he could to stem the tide of southern retributions against the Negro for having voted and held political offices during the Northern occupation. He tried to slow the process of Afro-American disenfranchisement by going along with the literacy qualification test. He knew the tactic would disqualify the majority of black voters, but thought the concession would serve as a firebreak to protect the literate ones. In that way, as each former bondsman learned to read and write he could join the rank of voting citizens.

Washington's campaign included writing letters to influential functionaries, planning conferences with important people, and talking to newsmen. He exhorted the southern power elite in the name of religion, compassion, justice, common decency, and political expediency. At one time Washington went so far as to have a former governor of West Virginia argue in his behalf at a public meeting. All his efforts failed, however. By 1910 Negroes in the South had been completely stripped of their right to vote.

20. Tuskegee's International Influence

Either the administration of a college or waging a civil rights campaign throughout the Confederacy would have been a full-time occupation for most men. But Washington managed these and had additional pots boiling and under control simultaneously. He played an important role in founding the Phelps-Stokes Fund established for the improvement of Negro education. And he was an influential voice in the expenditure of money from a number of other funds, of which the Peabody Fund and the Stater Fund were two of the most important.

On a more mundane level, Washington established and monitored a number of "how-to" programs around the rural environs of Tuskegee designed to help the inhabitants better their lives with the resources at hand. His programs included lectures complete with demonstrations, informal tests, and follow-up sessions. The how-tos consisted of the best methods of growing and harvesting peanuts, corn, sweet potatoes, and cotton, and the breeding, growing, butchering, and selling of hogs and cattle. He gave a complete course for the working farmer called the Farmer's Short Course, and he produced a *Farmer's Calendar* that included guidelines for plowing, planting, breeding, harvesting, sowing and reaping.

Washington's reputation for improving the lot of the dispossessed and bewildered of the earth and of making them self-sufficient and productive spread worldwide. In 1900 the German government asked Tuskegee Institute to introduce cotton agriculture into Togoland (at the time its African trust). Great Britain and   Bgium approached Tuskegee Institute with similar requests for their African trust territories. And two years later the Presbyterian Board of Foreign Missions requested that Tuskegee Institute introduce industrial education into China.

21. Du Bois's Development

William Du Bois, like Booker Washington, took his first steps along the leadership route by speaking *to* Negro youth. He began his career teaching at Fisk University. Unlike Douglass, who taught himself to read through furtive glances into a book concealed in his baggy clothing in an environment where Negro literacy was a crime, or

Washington, who was introduced to the alphabet by a circuit-riding teacher in middle Appalachia, Du Bois learned to read in a New England grammar school.

Before taking a position there as a teacher, Du Bois had attended Fisk a few years earlier as a student. Subsequently he had gone on to Harvard, then to the University of Berlin, and back to Harvard for his Ph.D. In the early stages of his career, he held the intellectual purist's conviction that evil was the result of ignorance. He believed that if he did enough research into the irrationality of racial prejudice and published his findings in a lucid manner, the best people of both races would join together in decisions that would supplant injustice with justice. So for the next three or four years he quietly taught his courses and plugged away at his research and writing, often having his articles published in some of the country's leading periodicals.

In time it began to occur to Du Bois that segregation and the abridgement of Negro rights were increasing rather than decreasing, contrary to what any logical timetable would require. The Emancipation Proclamation had been implemented more than a quarter-century before, and a number of creditable institutions of education for Negroes had been successfully operating in the South for almost as long. Political rights that Negroes had enjoyed during the northern occupation were evaporating like ground fog at sunrise, and the confederate state legislatures appeared to be in a race to see which could enact the newest and most ingeniously barbaric segregation statutes.

On different occasions Du Bois indicated that he could stomach educational and property qualifications for voting if they applied equally to both races and if blacks were provided with equal free school facilities. But he reasoned that if black schools were nonexistent or remained inferior to white schools, the likelihood of the masses ever gaining access to the voting booth through education was nil.

Du Bois argued that no one should expect the Negro to make the same advances in a couple of decades that it had taken the Anglo-Saxons a millennium to accomplish. No one was more aware than this increasingly dismayed scholar of history and sociology that the Europeans had thrashed about in moral and intellectual darkness for hundreds of years. The most successful ruffians and murderers had become the war lords and then the royalty. Even then the kings and queens played musical chairs with the thrones by chopping off the heads of the less devious claimants inside and outside their own families. And the practice did not diminish or cease until the Dark Ages ended with the founding of the universities.

At this point in his development and awareness, Du Bois began speaking *on behalf of* the Negro; not so much from the rostrum but through the articles he wrote. He was first, last, and always strictly intellectual—all statistics and footnotes. He thought the truly important things in life were ideas, concepts, and ideological models. He was also arriving at the conclusion that no group could secure its economic and cultural opportunities without its political rights. And it grieved him no end that Washington was going around the country speaking to overflowing audiences, downgrading the importance of voting and political rights.

Du Bois was convinced that the isolation of the Negro community from the national and international mainstream of thought and ideas emphasized the need for higher, rather than industrial, education. Only through higher education could the production of scholars and businessmen proceed. And slowly but surely he got his fill of the whole notion of industrial education.

22. The Genesis of the National Association for the Advancement of Colored People (NAACP)

Du Bois was as ruffled by Washington's philosophy as any of the anti-Tuskegee intellectuals in Boston, New York, or Washington. He was a teacher like Washington, however, in a southern institution. And despite himself he could see certain glittering facets of truth and logic here and there in the rough stone of Washington's pontifications. Yet Du Bois could never shake off the sense of uneasiness that Washington was sacrificing the promise of the race to the full belly, capering feet, and contented sleep of mediocrity.

Du Bois felt called upon to speak *for* the "talented tenth" in the Negro community. Since he had spoken *to* them for many years, and *on their behalf* for almost as long, his decision to speak *for* them rounded out his credentials as a full-scale leader.

Du Bois's malaise assumed the dimensions of despair at the turn of events following Washington's Atlanta speech in 1895. First there was the *Plessy v. Ferguson* Supreme Court decision. Using as the cornerstone of its rendition the phrase coined by Washington himself in describing the proper social relationship between whites and blacks, the Court announced its "separate but equal" doctrine of 1896. Then the President of the United States gave Washington a great deal of control, and almost absolute veto power, over Negro appointments in government.

Taken all together, Washington's power and prestige and what Du Bois considered to be his wrong-headed philosophy and compromising stance eventually became too much to endure. When he entered the fray against the Tuskegean, Du Bois's stature as a scholar and writer immediately catapulted him into the leadership role of the opposition to Washington's philosophy and what Du Bois dubbed the "Tuskegee Machine."

Du Bois realized that he would not have the massive following that Washington commanded. His message was not addressed exclusively to the ways and means of acquiring clothing, food, and farm land. He was making his pitch for the humanizing intangibles that man begins to contemplate only after having mastered the technique of providing for his basic needs. Du Bois believed that in a survival encounter, respect, if not victory itself, goes to the fighter rather than to the compromiser. In 1905 he met with a group of thirty other prominent Negroes in Fort Erie, Canada, and founded an organization that he called the Niagara Movement. By 1909 the Niagara Movement had acquired a number of white members who were sympathetic to the cause of Afro-American civil rights. In that year the Movement changed its name to the National Association for the Advancement of Colored People (NAACP). And being more of a writer than administrator, Du Bois gravitated to the position of editor of the *Crisis,* the NAACP's official publication.

With the *Crisis* and the wide popularity it enjoyed at his command, Du Bois intensified the campaign he had begun at the birth of the Niagara Movement. He launched an aggressive protest against the abridgement of civil rights, voting rights, and equal education opportunity, and an all-out war on Booker Washington's policies.

23. The Du Bois Philosophy

By the closing years of the first decade of the twentieth century, Du Bois had begun to view his campaign against Washington's philosophy and strategy as a holy obligation. He alone of Afro-American thinkers had access to the major opinion-making magazines and periodicals, as well as the *Crisis,* so he felt that the burden of proof of the Tuskegean's wrong-headedness was on his shoulders. And a heavy burden it was. Washington had both a national and international reputation as an educator, agriculturist, and leader extraordinary. He had access to the ears and checkbooks of the hard-headed northern industrialists who were favorably disposed to the causes of Negro uplift. He had the kind of political clout that only a minute number of whites and no Negroes ever contemplated in their wildest fantasies. And he had the stature, authority, and *élan vital* to enchant any audience—white, black, or integrated. Washington was successful, confident in the correctness of his philosophy, and he went about his work with the surly vigor of a cape buffalo. He was intimidating.

Du Bois kept up his scatter-gun attack, however, firing away with the special frustration that characterizes the theoretician's assault on the achieving activist. And despite the old saw that the pen is mightier than the sword, he saw his buckshot either miss its mark or bounce harmlessly off Washington's armor as the Tuskegean went unresponding and unperturbed about his business.

Du Bois attacked Washington for accommodating himself to the conditions of the times and place. Du Bois contended that no one should rest until the circumstances improved; that unless the social and political environment changed there should be no surcease of the vigor and volume of the protestation. He insisted that, unlike a peasant or an animal, a thinking man of character does not accept the landscape on which he finds himself, but strives to transform his surroundings into the pattern of his ideals. And even where significant changes are not readily attainable, one must look for signs of progress in his aspirations.

Du Bois attacked Washington for advocating aggressive self-help for the Negro rather than decrying injustice. He insisted that emphasis on self-help would permit the Southerner to shift the blame for the Negro's plight onto the shoulders of the Negro himself; that self-help was impossible when the full legal and moral force of an entire society were arrayed against an impotent and voteless minority. Besides, he did not believe that the Negro race had reached the point where donning the mantle of forgetting and forgiving was a becoming gesture. What was more, the sins against the race had never ceased. Clamoring and complaining unrelentingly about the obvious wrongs visited upon it would be a more fitting role.

When Washington advised Afro-Americans to spend less time seeking political appointments and more time developing industry and business, Du Bois joined the enraged intellectuals of the District of Columbia—whose *raison d'être* was the scramble for political appointments—to castigate Washington.

Du Bois and the Washingtonians interpreted the Tuskegean's advice as the ultimate ploy to the southern politician's ego. Here Washington seemed to be saying that not even the best minds in the Negro race should look beyond the aspirations of the *petite bourgeoisie*—beyond tilling the soil or hawking and haggling over the hand-to-hand exchange of a few grubby coins in the marketplace. He wanted to deny those of his race who were able the dignity of serving in the departments and bureaus that carried out the important and influential functions of the government and which conferred prestige on the participants.

The angry scholar came down on Washington for having suggested that the theorists knew a great deal about slavery in general but practically nothing about the feelings, needs, and gritty problems of the individual Negro. Du Bois accused Washington of black-belt parochialism, and of thinking small and in a way designed to please the confederate mentality, as usual.

The spectrum of Du Bois's emotional reaction to Washington, Washington's philosophy, and Washington's Tuskegee Machine ranged from violent anger through blue depression, and from green envy to red fear. And he was justified, from his frame of reference at any rate, on every count.

Du Bois was angry that Washington used his considerable talents of forthrightness, persuasion, and energy to promulgate a viewpoint of such limited scope. Anyone who cared to look could see that Washington's prescription for Afro-American success was destined to lead the entire race, including the "talented tenth," down the blind alley of mediocrity. What he advocated represented a reasonable goal for the masses at the time, but it portended maddening frustration for the talented. When pressed, however, Washington pointed out that he was working on behalf of the masses because the exceptional Negroes could fend for themselves. And that may have been an accurate statement of his aims, but his critics thought he was staking out such a definitive category for the Afro-American citizen that white America would not be likely to let any Negro cross the demarcation line between life's mundane concerns and higher aspirations. In short, Du Bois was livid that an individual as intelligent as Washington was so hell-bent on digging a pit for an entire race whose chance to escape grew more remote with each homily he preached and each concession he made.

It depressed Du Bois that Washington could meet with such massive success heading in the wrong direction, while he himself made such little headway following in the footsteps of all the advanced social thinkers since Socrates. It was as if the rules of humanity and civility that applied to the Greek and the Roman, and to the northern European, did not apply to the American of African extraction. Although he was leaving no word unsaid and no stone unturned it seemed that his philosophy was tacking against all the forces of American history and politics while Washington's was running confidently before the wind.

Finally there was the envy-and-fear end of the spectrum of Du Bois's feeling toward the Tuskegean. He could not escape the green monster's hot breath at the sight of his own principles being trampled under the heels of someone else's ideas—especially ideas careening off at such an ill-omened angle. The heft, authority, and unalloyed charisma that Washington brought to a speaker's platform was utterly discouraging. Whether the listeners were black or white, hoity-toity or hoi-polloi, made little difference. They practically ate from

Washington's hand. By contrast, Du Bois lacked the magnetism to fire the masses. His presentation was more suitable for the quiet room and the reading chair. His dignity and polish, reserve and sensitivity, robbed him of the quality that sets the troop commander apart from the expert witness or the cloistered speech writer.

Du Bois feared Washington's influence with the politicians and press, and with both the white citizens and black masses. He could literally feel Washington's power closing in upon him, shortening his breath and lengthening his frustration. Just as Du Bois could sense southern hostility to the Negro's quest for equality, education, and opportunity, he felt the black masses' dislike for discipline and learning, and their disdain for scholarship. And he felt that Washington was aiding and abetting these negative impulses. His was the rage and befuddlement with which the consumate theoretician ever beholds the prospering practical man.

Du Bois's deepest fear was of Washington's reputation for cutting down anyone who showed a potential for challenging his prominence. His own security was not a concern. His position as a scholar and writer was out of Washinton's reach. It was the younger fellows with talent and ambition who wanted to join him in the noble cause of freedom that Du Bois saw Washington's reputation terrorizing. It was they who needed scholarships, stipends, and recommendations. And in the Booker Washington era, nothing more than a stony silence from the groves of Tuskegee in response to an inquiry concerning the fitness and character of a Negro for what may have been a golden opportunity meant forever back to a life of menial pursuits. There was no way to measure the number of bright youngsters who would have been apprenticing in the vineyards of freedom had it not been for the menacing shadow of the Tuskegean. And without an oncoming crop of freedom fighters, Du Bois saw no hope for equality and justice for the Negro in his lifetime.

While his war of words against Washington had no discernible impact on the Tuskegean's stature, or on the deteriorating course of the Negro's position in the United States, Du Bois's anguish and frustration over the hopelessness of his campaign had the effect that a sense of losing often fosters in noble warriors. His unrealized hopes began to take on mystical dimensions.

Du Bois slowly developed a messianic vision of the Negro's role in society. He came to believe that every race had a message for the world. And since suffering, fasting, and plumbing the depths of the gloomy injustices of life have always been the harbingers of universal messages capable of turning the world around, he began to read a mission into the Negro's suffering. In his view the black race had not yet delivered its message. But Du Bois was convinced that if its best minds sought truth and worked and cooperated enthusiastically, the message could be designed and delivered to mankind.

Du Bois envisioned an ennobling black pride, an indomitable black solidarity, and a black, self-sufficient culture resulting from the struggle for this design. In time, the world would be as impressed and as eager to study the techniques and building blocks of black moral ascendancy as it was to study European law and technology and Eastern religions.

In line with his pursuits, Du Bois believed in parallel development for Negroes with full citizenship within the context of racial integrity and a self-imposed apartheid. He was not uncomfortable conceding that there had been a number of talented people who were derivatives of mixed stock. (The fathers of both Washington and Douglass were white.) He admitted to white blood in his own lineage (so much for the designation "black" rather than "colored" for the Afro-American) but it was Gallic; "not Teutonic, thank God."

Du Bois was adamant against racial intermarriage. He believed that such a relationship would tend to diffuse a Negro's focus on black solidarity, culture, and excellence. Besides, he never forgave the Anglo-Saxon for his willingness to share his posterity but not his prosperity.

Du Bois was more successful than he thought in pointing out and even magnifying the defects in Washington's work and philosophy. His attacks on the Tuskegean were so poignant and poetic that they outlasted the considerable positive aspects of Washington's works, and survived to be misused generations later as liturgical rejections of any thought to the self-examination that reason sometimes prescribes.

24. The Big Picture from Two Different Perspectives

Du Bois saw the big picture. He correctly perceived that a group
had no prospects of reaching its potential until it could avail itself
of the rights and opportunities of employment, education, public
accommodations, and legal justice that are available to free citizens.
He clearly understood that these rights had been withheld in different
degrees from various groups since the dawn of history, and that
rights are never bestowed but are "taken" in one way or another.
With his panoramic historical view he envisioned a grand strategy
befitting a five-star intellectual. His plan consisted of attacking the
bastions of oppression and injustice with chosen black knights dubbed
at his own "round table" and armed with broadswords and spears
of the sharpest intelligence—all tipped with unalloyed facts, statistics,
and self-evident truths.

In short, Du Bois envisioned a purely intellectual solution to
one of the most persistent and mundane dilemmas of mankind. Like
dreamers and mystics down through the ages, he worked out theories
and missions for the solutions of humanity's problems, complete
with a demonology. And in the process he left quotes to use, misuse,
or merely appear pedantic with.

Washington saw the big picture also, but his view was that of
an engineer rather than a designer. He understood racial stresses,
opportune moments, emotional friction, and social dynamics. Most
of all, he understood political lubricants and historical inertia. In
addition, he had the sure touch required to overcome the Newtonian
resistance of a massive project; to get it moving or bring it to rest,
as circumstances required. Washington could make things happen.

The picture Washington saw included a solution which a theoretician could see only in retrospect. This observation detracts nothing
from the theoretician. It reflects the fallacy of putting the cart before
the horse; of believing the conceptualization to be the working model.
If the two were identical, no need would exist for laboratory and
simulator tests—not to mention production and acceptance trials—
to plug the lethal incomprehensibles between concepts and functioning
mechanisms.

Washington's superiority lay in his comprehension of the need for the laboratory and simulator in the process of transforming the bondsman into the full citizen. He directed his energy toward raising the center of gravity of the black masses; toward starting a needed tradition of method, discipline, diligence, and self-sufficiency. He believed that pride and self-confidence stemmed from looking back at small accomplishments, thought out and executed against odds; that these personality characteristics grew as the accomplishments increased in scope and importance. He was convinced that a cadre of leaders trained in the skills of survival for the time and place where they found themselves and indoctrinated in the philosophy of progress by methodical steps could be sent among the masses and, in time, effect a complete racial uplift program.

Washington's faith in the process was such that he was unwilling to leave the start-up mechanics to hands other than his own. He thought that with the center of mass of black people functioning on an ever-higher plane of enlightenment, they would in time acquire a bedrock of hope, ambition, and confidence. In his opinion, random talent and brains were as likely to spring up from the masses as from the privileged classes. He was convinced that, with the majority of the race gradually lifted out of its hopeless state and working, aspiring, and striving for self-betterment, the chance of grooming scholars and professionals would be better than concentrating black hope on the few advantaged Negroes who existed at the turn of the century.

Washington hoped to effect a Negro momentum in the direction of community order and excellence rather than toward individual stardom—often predicated on luck and breaks. And had his prescription been fulfilled, today's Afro-American elementary schools would have been beehives of excellence in reading, writing, and arithmetic, and, later, in commercial education, chemistry, and calculus—pursuits a technological labor force can absorb.

Had Washington's time and temperament permitted him to spell out his plans to Du Bois in a convincing way, or had Du Bois's pride and paranoia permitted him to perceive the validity of Washington's plan, the two titans could have pulled in tandem. They could have wrought a tradition of Negro aspiration and scholarship that would have changed the contours and dimensions of America. The Afro-American would have had the opportunity to merge into the mainstream of the country's life without the aid of fire torches from the gritty ghettos, where the vast outpouring of energy was channelled through rebellious rather than constructive and progressive avenues.

THE NEGRO PRESS

25. The Genesis of the Negro Press

No commentary on Afro-American leadership in its Golden Century would be complete without a respectful tip of the hat to the Negro press. That institution fulfilled the leadership requirement in every respect. It spoke *on behalf of* the Negro, *for* the Negro, and *to* the Negro. It was the advocate, the voice, and the mentor of the Afro-American citizen. While the printed word lacked the benefits of face-to-face exchange and the immediate clarification of ideas, it had compensating advantages. Its area of coverage was much wider than any speaker could hope to achieve. It could be passed from reader to reader until worn out, and it could be read repeatedly and discussed endlessly. Also, it could be filed away and referred to time and again. Finally, a newspaper could be concealed and smuggled into places where individuals advocating the same ideas or carrying similar messages would be made short work of by the forces opposing their stance.

Negro newspapers were born in protest—protest against slavery and the injustices inflicted against free Negroes. They did not stop with protest, however; they donned the mantle of full leadership from the first printing.

In the first paragraph of its introduction, the first issue of the first Negro newspaper published in the United States vowed to disseminate useful knowledge. In the third paragraph it promised to denounce misconduct. And the entire fourth paragraph was devoted to a discussion of the value of education. It spoke of education in terms of concentrated effort, and warned against trivial pursuits.

The editor was James Russwurm. He joined with Samuel Cornish in New York City to establish the publication. The newspaper was called *Freedom's Journal,* and its mission was clearly what its name implied.

Within the three decades following the birth of *Freedom's Journal*, a number of Negro newspapers sprang up bearing such purposeful names as *Weekly Advocate, Colored American, Elevator, National Watchman, Genius of Freedom, Ram's Horn, North Star, Colored Man's Journal,* and *Herald of Freedom.*

In addition, numerous protest pamphlets and circulars were printed and distributed among Afro-Americans, which helped crystallize their thoughts and viewpoints. One such circular, which had a life span of only four issues, was printed by David Walker in Boston. Walker had lived in North Carolina most of his life, and his writings reflected his rage and resolve to do what he could about slavery. His pamphlet had wide circulation in 1827, and created such an upsetting effect among slaveholders in the Southeast that the mayor of Savanna petitioned the mayor of Boston to arrest and punish Walker. The state of Virginia considered Walker's circulars seditious literature, and the mayor of Boston was inclined to agree with the southern position. At any rate, a fifth edition of the circular never appeared, but history does not indicate what action, if any, the mayor of Boston took against Walker.

In January 1837, the *Weekly Advocate,* advocating suffrage, knowledge, and refinement, introduced itself to the Afro-American community. In its second issue a week later, it vowed to expose the kidnappers of hundreds of the quarter-million free Negroes who lived in the North. The same editorial promised to impart useful and moral instruction.

In May of the same year, the *Colored American* stated that the greatest deficiency of the colored American was the lack of opportunity to cultivate his intellect with extensive and solid knowledge.

In December 1847, Frederick Douglass's paper, the *North Star,* appeared on the scene in Rochester, New York. It stated as its purposes improving the morality and intelligence of the colored people and hastening the freedom of the three million bondsmen. Another of the principal objectives of the *North Star* was to change the nation's view of the Negro's supposed inferiority.

In April 1853, the *Alienated American* introduced itself to the colored citizens of Cleveland, Ohio. Among its purposes, it proposed to represent the colored Americans, and to aid them in their educational development and in their acquisition of industrial skills.

In July 1859, the *Weekly Anglo-African* indicated in its inaugural editorial its intention to set forth the course of the Afro-American clearly and to create a sense of community. It vowed to direct its readers' attention toward industry, self-reliance, and education.

And in March of 1865, the *New Orleans Tribune* declared that the equal treatment of colored soldiers and a common school for colored children were two of the planks in its platform.

26. The Negro Press during the Years of Slavery

During the years before the Civil War every southern plantation of any consequence was populated by many more blacks and mulattoes than whites. The bourbons clearly understood that the maintenance of bourbon law and order was dependent upon keeping a tight psychological rein on the slave population. The bondsman had to be convinced of his good fortune in having someone provide him with food and shelter in return for his labor and protect him from the evils of the complex world as long as his good conduct and loyalty warranted them. The logical extension of this concept was that the slave was a dependent, mentally inferior human. Moreover, he was untrustworthy and needed close supervision.

In their zeal to convince the slaves of their inability to cope on their own, the planters also convinced themselves that the bondsmen were hopelessly retarded as a class. This conviction was no great feat considering the motivation. The entire confederate infrastructure of privilege and leisure rested upon the slave economy. And once the bitter hoax was in place and subscribed to by all concerned, reality for the bondsman became the recognition of his own subnormality.

If by word or deed, purposely or mistakenly, he contradicted his betters, it was the bondsman who was wrong—no matter in which direction the facts pointed. If he did not show enthusiasm for toiling from sunup to sundown, then he was unappreciative of the provisions made for him. And heaven forbid if he talked or even thought of escaping the unremitting toil that was his fate until death; this was the ultimate proof of his unreliability.

Within the context of slavocracy it was a crime to teach a bondsman to read. The prohibition was never completely effective, however. Humans being humans, many of the bourbon children and slave children developed childhood friendships and learned to read together. In numerous other cases white women taught certain of their house servants to read. The deed was sometimes motivated by the conviction on the part of the chatelaine that anyone who wanted to learn to read was entitled to be taught. At other times the motivation sprang from a religious fervor to enable another human to read the Bible for the salvation of both souls concerned. And human emotions being what they are, some slaves were taught to read out of pique against a baronial system in which the lady in the big house lived in a genteel bondage only slightly less restrictive than that imposed on her servants, while the lord of the manor often philandered all over, often including liaisons with the upstairs bondswomen.

Even the baron himself frequently winked at the reading prohibition, in view of the fact that some of the younger house servants were often of his own blood. And as sure as a few of the in-house slaves here and there mastered the art, some, in turn, had their own reasons for teaching the technique to a brother or sister in the field now and then.

It was within this social atmosphere that the pre-Civil War Negro newspapers and pamphlets caused so much consternation in the South. Even purely Christian publications from colored organizations were looked upon as dangerous documents. The few slaves who could read, and who by hook or by crook came into possession of any of the papers or pamphlets, digested the good news and innovative ideas and put the word on the eager grapevine. The news, notions, and ideas passed by word of mouth in the kitchens and fields, and through the dark shanties at night. They crescendoed into a community of thought, purpose, and potential beyond anything an observer outside the poor communications system of the sparsely settled Southland could imagine.

From the time the first newspapers and pamphlets began filtering

into Dixie, tension between the bourbons and the bondsmen assumed
the strains of a force field. No community was without its volunteer
militia and patrols. Even so, during the thirty-seven years between
1827 and 1864 there were more than 120 substantial slave conspiracies
and revolts of record. One suspects that an equal number of plots
and uprisings went unrecorded. And it is easy to agree with the
popular belief at the time that the pamphlets that circulated the
accounts of Toussaint L'Ouverture in Haiti in the 1790s, and of
Gabriel Prosser and Denmark Vesey in the 1800s, produced the kind
of consciousness-raising among the bondsmen that made Nat Turner's
exploit possible.

From its establishment in 1827 until the Civil War, the Negro
press was the only nationally unifying instrument in the Afro-
American community. Distances were measured by stagecoach,
horseback, and ox-cart. These modes of travel placed Washington,
D.C., and Baltimore forty miles apart, more distant time-wise than
Washington and London are now by modern transportation. Prior
to the Civil War, had it not been for the Negro newspapers, a free
Negro in Philadelphia would have been as remote from a slave in
his quarters on a Georgia plantation as an Earthling is from an
inhabitant of outer space. But with the newspapers, the two often
shared the same interpretation of events that affected them both,
and the same coalition of thoughts, desires, and aspirations.

27. The Negro Press following the Civil War

At the conclusion of the Civil War the former slaves were obsessed
with the desire to learn to read. Having previously been forbidden
literacy, they correctly associated ignorance with bondage. Endless
accounts are recorded of Negroes of all ages pouring over hard-
to-come-by readers, Bibles, and spelling books. They studied by
candlelight in cabins and by firelight in the woods at night. Miners
even struggled with the alphabet by flickering bank lamps in the
salt and coal mines.

The Negro press was as ready for this vast new clientele as
the new readers were for the press. The papers' themes included
the evils of Jim Crow, the Negro's rights under the Constitution,

and Negro self-respect, conduct, and behavior. They gave wide coverage to incidents of racism, and reported on numerous trumped-up charges against Negroes which had little or nothing to do with any actual crime.

For seventy or more years following the Civil War, varying from location to location, Negroes who did not yield the sidewalk or pathway to whites who wanted the right of way, who stood their ground in arguments, or who were not quite docile enough to conform to the mores were charged with statutory crimes. Added to the list of those wrongfully charged were others who seemed too prosperous, too ambitious, or who had unwarranted aspirations for their children.

In certain times and places Afro-Americans were unduly punished for sassing, drunkenness, fighting, disturbing the peace, loitering, vagrancy, and larceny. But the most fiendishly refined charge was "rape." Rape hit the emotional jackpot. It was the ultimate catch-all. The crime could not be defended, and no proof was required. The charge itself was enough to trigger the ancestral touchstone of delicious horror of the entire Confederacy. It picked at the decorative thread perennially woven in the cloth of European literature. The theme betrayed the male's subliminal sexual anxieties and his simultaneous enjoyment of the self-inflicted torture derived from imagining the violation of his platinum womanhood by some beastly subhuman. At the dawn of Western civilization there were Europa and the Bull, and Leda and the Swan—immortalized centuries later by great Renaissance art. Subsequently European literature treated the male to the *Tales from the Arabian Nights.* The universality of the obsession was authenticated in the way that *primus inter pares* of English language writers portrayed a conniver taunting Desdemona's father, "Your daughter and the Moor are now making the beast with two backs." Twentieth-century America's version consisted of Tarzan's Jane being carried away to a fate "a thousand times worse than death" by Terkoz, the great bull ape who had been one of Tarzan's childhood playmates and who became his mortal enemy in maturity. And, finally, there was King Kong.

The Negro press hammered relentlessly at all charges it determined to be false or questionable. It called for federal investigations and laws to redress overt travesties of justice. It regularly reported Afro-American progress in employment, business, and education, and took special pride in the accounts of activities surrounding the colleges. Great emphasis was accorded their social life and athletic enterprises.

The preponderance of Negroes lived in poverty or slightly above its demarcation line for the first three-quarters of a century following Emancipation. Travel was a luxury which only a few could afford. Without access to the ten-cent Negro weekly, those in the country's hamlets, byways, and wide spots in the road would have known little or nothing of the great Afro-American colleges with their professors, doctors, lawyers, ministers, football teams, and homecoming queens. The press also kept an account of Negro migration from the poverty-ridden rural South to the comparative heaven of freedom and employment opportunity in the North.

28. The Value of the Negro Press

The early Negro press sailed perpetually in precarious financial waters. Advertising was scant and credit practically nonexistent. Who could expect an establishment banker to lend money to an organ whose *raison d'être* was attacking the establishment of which he was the cornerstone? The editors toiled on, however, against the odds. For the most part they were men dedicated to the cause for which they were fighting. They put their mission above profit. And while Negro papers were more expensive than white papers of equal size and coverage, their readers still considered them bargains. How else could they come by "race news," keep up their hope and faith that life would become better by and by, and keep in touch with the country's leading Afro-American thinkers?

29. The Negro Press at Its Apex

Between the Civil War and World War I, a number of significant Negro newspapers arrived on the scene. They included the *Philadelphia Tribune* in 1884, the *New York Age* in 1885, and the *Afro-American* in 1892. The turn of the century brought the *Norfolk Journal and Guide* in 1900, the *Chicago Defender* in 1905, the

Amsterdam News in 1909, and the *Pittsburgh Courier* in 1910. Many others were established across the country during this period and later. Some of them are still on the newsstands in the 1980s.

The circulation of Negro newspapers in the United States in the early 1920s was approximately one million. The readership was estimated to be five million. This number included the families of the purchasers, secondhand readers, borrowers, and individuals who sat in group readings.

More than 450 such newspapers were said to be in print in the decade of the 1920s. Some were devoted to religion, others to business, and still others were music publications. And there were also the usual college newspapers. But the preponderance of the publications fell into the "race papers" class.

It was also in the 1920s that the Negro newspapers overtook the pulpit in influence with the Afro-American masses. They voiced their preoccupation with the problems of Negroes, and correctly pointed out that the white press played up Negro crime and played down Negro achievement. And they set about to create a temporary colored civilization within the white civilization until the time came when a just merger was possible. They strove to crystallize Negro thought around subjects crucial to the welfare of the race. Their purposes were to project Negroes in a good light and to instill in them the self-esteem necessary to bear up with dignity under the institutionalized social and legal humiliations which defined the perimeters of their lives.

In their mentor role the newspapers continued to denounce improper conduct, extol the value of promptness, and decry the ill-repute which the crimes of a few members brought down on the entire race. They continued firing away at the evils of gambling, the undesirability of creating slums, and the virtues of cleanliness—even to the point of denouncing the habit practiced in some churches of drinking sacramental wine from a common bowl. As for etiquette, as late as the early 1950s the *Pittsburgh Courier* took a group of ladies of that city to task for attending baseball games—to see Jackie Robinson play—dressed in the kind of heels and flimsy finery usually reserved for soirées.

The newspapers counseled the display of Negro pictures and

portraits in Negro homes. They also advised against one Negro betraying another who decided to "pass" for white for the advantages being white accrued. There was always the chance, somewhere down the road, that a good word or deed might be rendered still another Negro out of remembrance. The papers believed that taking the long view was better than acting maliciously toward a brother out of the jealous belief that he was abandoning the brotherhood.

One newspaper, the *Buffalo American,* kept at the head of its editorial column a guide to behavior which it called the "Oath of Afro-American Youth." It began with "I will," and it included a pledge "never to bring disgrace to the race by deed or act." It promised to live a clean and decent life and to respect, defend, and honor womanhood. It vowed to uphold and obey the just laws of the country and community, and to encourage others to do likewise. It promised never to let injustice cow or sour the soul, and it pledged self-improvement and racial responsibility.

30. Tribulations of the Negro Press

As a crusading organ, the Negro press suffered the wrath reserved for crusaders. And because the crusade was racial in a racist region there was a special venom in the wrath. It received hundreds of letters and threats, many from the Ku Klux Klan, and almost as many from outraged unassociated citizens. The messages usually contained stern advice and dire warnings. The papers were advised that their positions on voting, employment, and integration were improper nonsense to be advocating for an unprepared race. They were told that if the nonsense continued, everyone concerned, especially the newspaper, would suffer the retribution they deserved.

In the violence-prone, racist atmosphere of the first sixty years following Emancipation, these threats were more than empty rhetoric. A number of offices where southern newspapers were printed and distributed were burned between 1900 and the end of the 1920s. Northern newspaper distributors were sometimes arrested and sometimes chased out of town. In some instances individuals were murdered for distributing Negro newspapers.

More than one southern governor blamed northern Negro

newspapers for Negro unrest and rioting. A number of cities, burgs, and counties enacted laws prohibiting the publication or circulation of demands for racial equality. One of the angriest accusations against the Negro press was that it caused a labor crisis in some farm districts. By indicating that there were better job opportunities elsewhere it decimated the black labor force, its detractors said. Matters degenerated to such an intolerable state that owners of some of the large farms were subject to the humiliation of having to put their own hands to the plow.

31. The Widening Influence of the Negro Press

Over the years, the scope of the Negro newspaper crusade widened. Editors and publishers were developing the business acumen needed to make their enterprises paying propositions. As literacy approached national proportions and majority citizens other than its enemies began to read the Afro-American press in significant numbers, the organs developed new clout.

The Negro press began demanding better education and better facilities in Afro-American public schools. Through words and pictures they pointed up hundreds of inequalities in facilities. In every southern and border state scores of graphic examples could be shown of the dilapidated little Negro schoolhouses, sometimes propped up with poles, in juxaposition with the modern white learning centers. The names were usually "City" or "Burg High School" for the whites, and "City" or "Burg Colored High School" for the Negroes. The sorry arrangements showed the interpretations that the various town fathers and boards of education gave the U.S. Supreme Court's 1896, *Plessy v. Ferguson,* "separate but equal" decision. It had become a cause with the Afro-American press to remind the country without surcease that the phrase "separate but equal" had in reality become "separate and unequal." The inequality even extended to black versus white teachers' salaries. "Teaching" Negroes was not considered as worthy an occupation as "educating" whites. And that state of affairs became another bone of contention for the colored press.

In addition to its education crusade, the Negro press kept up a drumfire of agitation for black suffrage in the former confederate states. And they also ran a parallel harangue against the eligible Afro-Americans who did not register and vote in the states where they were permitted to do so.

By the 1920s and 1930s self-respecting Negroes considered it racially sacrilegious not to vote. Their press had convinced them that voting for liberal candidates was the principal means open to them for aiding their cause and the cause of their more unfortunate brothers and sisters in states where Negroes were not yet permitted the ballot.

The Negro press first seriously tried its wings on the employment winds in Afro-American neighborhoods where white-owned businesses were located. It rightly calculated that enterprises dependent on Negro patronage were more susceptible to the clamor for better jobs than businesses with no such dependence. There they set forth the idea of boycotts with the phrase "Don't buy where you can't work." It was years later, after larger firms recognized the Afro-American buying potential, that boycott thrusts were made against businesses located outside of Negro neighborhoods.

32. The Negro Press during World War II

In the receding years of the 1930s, when the war clouds over Europe hung threateningly on America's remote horizons, the country began tooling up to aid its allies. In 1941, war became an American reality. Every citizen was called upon to either bear arms or exert himself unstintingly to produce war-related material in the name of patriotism, freedom, and democracy.

A crisis is a turning point at which either great gains accrue, or all is lost. The outcome depends upon the mode of crisis management employed by those involved. The Afro-American press recognized in the national crisis an opportunity to advance the Negro's cause. It sprang at the chance. Its philosophy had been in place for decades and its techniques in the process of refinement since the early 1920s. First they took up the cudgel for equal training and employment opportunity. Such a thrust could hardly fail to make gains. There was a shortage of war material, of quality food, of fuel and clothing, and of labor. It bordered on insanity, the press contended, to bar a tenth of the workforce from critical sectors of employment based upon racist traditions. Racism as usual ill-served both the majority and the minority citizen, and their common concern with the war effort as well. The Negro press drumrolled this line of reasoning loudly, clearly, and continuously. Like any master salesman or politician, it cast its demands within the matrix of what the country wanted: to win the war as quickly as possible with minimal loss of its sons and natural resources.

With equal enthusiasm and patriotic justification, the Negro press set out in pursuit of desegregation of the armed forces and demanded combat roles for Negro servicemen.

Negroes had always engaged at the combat level in America's wars, from Crispus Attucks—a black who was the first to give his life in the Revolutionary War—onward. But a great deal of confusion had been consistently generated around the Afro-American soldier's official role. Negro combat troops participated in the Civil War and in World War I. The entire 369th Infantry regiment, an all-Negro unit, was awarded the French *Croix de Guerre*. Private Henry Johnson of that regiment was the first American ever to receive the medal. Yet the national orthodoxy held that Negroes were too excitable and fearful to make good combat troops. They were thought to be better suited for construction and service duties. In the racist atmosphere of the 1920s immediately following World War I, most of the discharged white soldiers who spoke for the record insisted that they had never seen Negroes in combat, and that on the rare occasions when their service units were threatened by Germans, the black troops had run like frightened rabbits.

At the beginning of World War II the Marine Corps, a voluntary unit and the most celebrated American combat arm, did not accept Negroes. The Navy used Negroes only as stewards. And the Army Air Corps had no Negroes in its ranks. So, hard on the heels of its equal employment opportunity campaign, the Negro press turned its verbal fusillade on segregation in the armed services. Week after week after week it shrieked with one voice for integration of the armed forces, the assignment of Negro troops to combat duty, the training of Negroes for air crew duty, and the promotion of Negroes to higher ranks. The clamor was sometimes adroitly embroidered with the noble sentiments of freedom, justice, and democracy, which the national press and politicians employed to rouse the nation and the world against totalitarian injustice. And sometimes the themes of segregation and the lack of equality were played in counterpoint to the country's virtuous wartime pronouncements.

A number of the more prominent newspapers sent war correspondents to monitor the Negro soldiers' treatment and conduct in battle zones around the globe. They filed countless stories of discrimination and racial strife, and gave a number of dramatic accounts of false accusations made against Negro soldiers reminiscent of the method of bringing "uppity" blacks to heel in the Confederacy.

The Negro newspapers did not let the fact that the higher echelons of the armed services were tilted southward go unnoticed. This resulted from the tradition of better opportunities in business and the professions for ambitious men in the North than existed in the South. Consequently, far more Southerners than Northerners found the armed services attractive and even romantic. Besides, an armed services career provided one of the few legitimate ways to recapture bourbonism.

In more than one case, the Negro press raised an unholy furor about instances of brutality inflicted upon Negro soldiers in the armed services. It named the theaters, the times, and the ranks of the officers and enlisted men involved. It pointed out the disparity between the American theory of justice and the black reality so graphically that some of the more rabid custodians of the racial status quo in Congress regenerated the time-honored old saw of sedition. They threatened darkly of investigations and subpoenas, and of charges in the making against certain of the newspapers.

The seditionist balloon never flew, however. The Negro press had proclaimed its Americanism. Every demand and appeal it presented was based on the Constitution and was made in its name and spirit. It always stated clearly that it wanted its cases handled in the United States courts under the same procedures that mainline America's cases were handled. It demanded Afro-American rights in the name and within the context of Americanism. Time and again it had confirmed that the Afro-American's salvation was inextricably bound up with the salvation of America. The tradition was forthright and on public display for anyone who cared to inspect it. So the Negro press was in a position to attack the sedition-mongers with all the indignation of the wounded righteous. And they took advantage of every opportunity until the seditionist mumbling was muted.

The Negro newspapers played the role of the free press to the hilt. The times were abristle with the righteous purpose of eradicating the Nazi hideosity from the face of the earth for all ages. Under the circumstances, the government was keenly aware of and justifiably embarrassed about the validity of the contrasts which the Negro papers pointed out between its preachings and practices as they applied to the most conspicuous of its minority citizens. It was a few days following an incident in which one of the President's trusted advisors lost his composure and physically attacked a member of the Negro press corps that an Afro-American Army officer was first promoted to the rank of brigadier general. Considering the timing, the feeling was widespread in the Negro community that the promotion was effected to deflect the laser beam of outrage directed at the guilty official by the Negro press.

Not every Afro-American was enthusiastic about its press's campaign to thrust Negroes into combat. Many of the soldiers in question, standing as they were at the fork of the road between rustling up supplies and rushing machine gun nests, would have chosen the former had they been given a plebiscite. In many of the far-flung segregated barracks and quonset huts around the world, the newspapers were hardly more welcome than they were in a Dixiecrat congressional office.

But the journals took the long view. They knew that a government whose claim to uniqueness rested on the posture it struck before the world and its own mirror could not long deny justice to those of its citizens who had borne arms for its principles. The Negro press took the Puritan ethic stance. They were willing to purchase their ticket before expecting entrance into the justice and equal opportunity arena. And throughout the parallel campaigns for employment and an opportunity to defend America, they enjoined the Afro-American to throw a full measure of effort into the enterprise and to expect a full measure of freedom, justice, and opportunity in return. Their persistent theme hoisted the banner of expectation in the Negro community.

Thus while our European allies and the mainline American held up the index and middle fingers to symbolize a V for victory, the Negro press advocated a double V: one for the expeditionary forces, and a second for the triumph of justice for the Afro-American at home.

And just as there was considerable white sympathy for the Negro predicament predating the birth of the nation and an equal sentiment afoot throughout the abolitionist period, there was enough such empathy alive to make its weight felt during World War II. The pre-Revolutionary War sentiment was summed up in Abigail Adams's letter to her husband in September 1774, when she empathized that the slaves "have as good a right to freedom as we have." She had no trouble with the parallel between the relationships of the Colonists and the British, and the Negroes and the Colonists. The very name of the era speaks for the abolitionist period. And the anti-discrimination initiatives, which began with President Roosevelt's Fair Employment Practices Commission in 1941 and culminated in President Johnson's Voting Rights Act in 1965, spoke for the times which represented the Negro press's finest hour.

33. The Negro Press in Decline

Specialized inventions, such as crossbows, swords, stagecoaches, and crusading newspapers, come on the scene and serve their ages brilliantly in the advancement of civilization. But in time, like hobby horses on a carousel, they rotate and disappear into a din of noise and confusion. During the century and a half between its ascent and its eclipse in the decade of the 1960s, the Negro press both preceded and survived the leadership of Douglass, Washington, Du Bois, and many other notable Negro teachers, spokesmen, and advocates. It was an entity consisting of hundreds of dynamic segments, all exerting their efforts in a common direction, all coordinated by a single-minded urgency to improve the lot of Afro-Americans on their native soil. Its deeds and consequences could not bring it the hero worship and personal identification accorded living, breathing individuals. But its contributions to Afro-American progress were immeasurable. It is impossible to imagine how segregated trains, busses, and classrooms, not to mention better employment opportunities and equal sacrifices in the armed forces, could have happened without the role the Negro press played in U.S. history. Its influence was certainly greater than that of any single individual.

The fact that the Negro press followed historical patterns of rise and decline subtracts nothing from its illustrious leadership life cycle. It is still alive after a fashion, but so is the ceremonial sword and the sidetracked passenger coach. The functions of the Negro press are different now. It would be the first to admit that it is only a shadow of the tower of influence it was in the 1930s and 1940s.

A specialized organism depends upon its environment for survival. Novel factors and complex attitudes arose in the sixties to end the hegemony of the Negro press: the passage of new civil rights legislation on the one hand, and the emergence of new civil rights functionaries with their open disdain for traditional Negro leadership on the other. According to the new litany, blacks had not gotten out of the back of the bus because of traditional black leadership. They accused their elders of being too reasonable, logical, and patient, when only a boisterous confrontation could obtain results. Living solely in the "now" as they did, the new functionaries never perceived that the backdrop before which their tactics worked had been woven painstakingly, strand by strand, over more than a dozen decades. And non-readers that they were, it never occurred to them that bondsmen and second-class citizens had confronted injustice from the 1600s onward. The uprisings had been crushed with violence and paid for in blood, and without the meticulously woven backdrop, the series of protests in the sixties would have suffered the same fate. The neophytes came on the scene when the climate was right for action. They acted and achieved results, but without any manifestation of the Newtonian humility which prompted the genius to observe that he was able to see so far afield because he had stood on the shoulders of giants. They arrogated all credit to themselves with shrill voices and raised fists. And the television cameras who feed on sensationalism and nonsense were there to publically authenticate their claims.

In such a cacophonous atmosphere any voice of reason sounded like a whimper. The Afro-American press, like every other coherent voice, suddenly found itself irrelevant, if not counter-revolutionary. It had to back off from its role as mentor. The new functionaries were having none of it. Survival required that the press align itself with the times. News, entertainment, and advertisement copy were now all it had left. Its days of leadership and its finest hours were over—and at just the point in time when a majority of its constituency, lurching aimlessly about in a new climate of freedom, needed leadership more than ever.

Chapter 4
AFRO-AMERICAN LEADERSHIP AND EDUCATION

1. The Degeneration of Afro-American Elementary Education

An article of faith of the meek states that the punishment will fit the crime. If the adage is worth the breath that whimpering it requires, with glittering exceptions the destiny of modern elementary teachers and school administrators in J's community is a special brand of brimstone. Their mode of blasé, disgruntled, and confused teaching has not always prevailed, however. A generation or so ago, classrooms were learning centers rather than nuclei of confusion and apology. They were teacher-centered rather than child-centered; adult-directed rather than in a state of puerile chaos and drift.

When only a few professions were open to Negroes, the cream of the crop went into teaching. The individuals took seriously their work and the responsibility of molding the young minds entrusted to their custody. The education process had not yet become an arcane network connecting distorting nodes of parents, politicians, sociological and psychological hired guns, and diverse pressure groups with the needs of the individual pupil lost in its intricacies. The process would not have become an intimidating octopus of confusion to the caliber of individuals who had the first crack at teaching Afro-American children, at any rate. They were too intelligent and confident in what they were about. The transmission of a body of knowledge from a mature mind to a young one was something they recognized as a reasonably straightforward process. The mechanics consisted of introducing a concept, demonstrating the method for its reproduction, and drilling until the method was memorized and perfected. While no one ever thought so simple an approach was the sum and substance of teaching, it was recognized as the beginning necessity. The display-demonstration-drill method constitutes step one. Without it, ascending the golden stairs of learning is either delayed, negotiated insecurely, or never accomplished at all.

At the introductory juncture of a subject there is no room for discussion and the exchange of ideas. The pupil has no ideas to exchange, nor does he have sufficient knowledge about the subject to ask questions. And pretending that he does is detrimental flattery which should not be imposed upon him.

Application of the display-demonstration-drill method is not restricted to the alphabet and multiplication tables, which were discussed earlier. It represents the start-up technique for any subject one hopes to pursue with success. The rules of English grammar must be memorized long before they become articles of question, discussion, and philosophy. When early presentation, drill, and reinforcement throughout elementary school are disregarded, the neglected students have obvious trouble with their language. They wear the logo of the disadvantaged all the days of their lives.

The study of algebra is another example of how the basic concepts of a subject must be mastered before satisfactory progress can be made. The distinction between known and unknown quantities must be presented and the rules for solving equations memorized. Without memorizing the rules—the knowns and unknowns must be collected on opposite sides of the equal sign and added, and both sides of the equation divided by the coefficient of the unknown—a student will stand forever intimidated before an algebraic equation. Once the basic equation is practiced and mastered through drill, one is ready for factoring, graphing, quadratics, systems of equations, word problems, exponents and radicals, and the method of least squares, etc. If the student failed to master the technique of the simple equation, he will have been lost for weeks by the time "the method of least squares and related topics" is presented.

Two other courses which may be used as examples to be undertaken by way of memorization, if progress within a reasonable time frame is the objective, are calculus and airplane pilotage.

In an introduction to calculus, one must review everything pre-viously learned about variables and functions and clear up any vague notions about their relations and notations. The student must acquire a thorough grasp of continuity and the idea of limits. After a few days of drill with examples involving limits, he is introduced to differen-tiation and given the general rule to memorize. Then follows an exhaus-tive number of examples in which the rule is applied. By this time it has occurred even to the new student that differentiation by the general rule is labor intensive and error prone. So it is back to the learner's fundamental tool: memorization. The student must memorize the rules for differentiating algebraic and transcendental functions, and parametric and polar equations. If these rules are not memorized thoroughly, one's progress in differential calculus soon grinds to a halt; if they are memorized, then it is on to integral calculus—and the same learning process.

An interest in learning to pilot an airplane, again, like learning anything of value, requires the start-up memorization of a considerable catalogue of facts, rules, and formulas.

Before one is allowed inside the aircraft he has to memorize the names and functions of the controls, the three axes around which the vehicle rotates, and how these are related. Then the definitions and meanings of *camber, lift, drag, roll, pitch,* and *yaw,* must be learned. Once inside, one must memorize the steps required to accomplish the series of basic maneuvers designed to impart a "feel" for the aircraft. Following hours of drill on the maneuvers, one is ready to practice "shooting" landings in preparation for his first solo (flying without an instructor) flight. Again memorization is in order. It includes the rotation speed, climb-out speed, pattern headings, and cruise speed. Preparation for landing requires memorizing the flap positions on different legs of the pattern, and the approach and landing speeds. And the go-around procedure must be memorized so thoroughly that its application is unalloyed reflex (just as the answer to "six-times-seven" should have been since the fifth grade).

The student pilot must learn all the signs, symbols, and definitions of a sectional chart. Skillful use of the navigation plotter and computer must be developed. All the symbols used in weather charts and reports must be engraved in the cranium. One must memorize the various cloud formations, their causes, and what type of weather accompanies each. Then there are the definitions for true headings, magnetic headings, compass headings, and the way they are related to wind drift and magnetic variation to be learned. In addition, there are radio procedures, controlled airport approach and departure procedures, and emergency (including fire, ice, and engine-out) procedures to be memorized so well that any one of them may be recalled posthaste.

At various times this writer has seen youngsters approach the above pursuits, give what they considered their best try, then quit in frustration, often furious at their instructor. Either calculus or airplane pilotage can be grasped by nineteen of twenty individuals of average intelligence. Disappointment at an attempt to learn one of them is based upon a single disability: the failure to recognize that the first step in learning is memorization.

As late as the 1930s people accepted the reality of competition as a fact of life. Afro-American grammar school teachers applied this reality unphilosophically. They were not psychologists, sociologists, or education theorists. They had finished grade school, high school, and at least two years of college. This gave them a thorough grounding in arithmetic, spelling, English grammar, American literature, geography, and history. They had an excellent working knowledge of algebra, Latin, and nature study, and had done a great deal of reading. All of them could sing the usual songs children were expected to learn in school, and many could play the piano. With a sense of mission they simply passed along the knowledge they had in a straightforward, no-nonsense, unapologetic, uncomplicated manner.

In many schools an entire section of the class in reading and spelling stood in a line in front of the room to "recite" the lesson. There was an audience because the remainder of the class was still seated and paying rapt attention. Students had the opportunity every day to appear either "smart" or "dumb" before their peers. Under the circumstances, the incentive to learn was off to an early start— especially if the audience included a little girl or boy on whom one wanted to make a favorable impression, or, in front of whom, at least, one did not want to appear stupid.

The line had a head and a foot. One's position in the line was based upon one's demonstrated ability to read or spell, as the case required. The pupil at the head of the reading class on a given day could read faster and understand and explain the meaning of a lesson better than anyone else. The person in the second position could read, understand, and explain second best. This pattern prevailed all the way to the foot of the class where the lowest achiever was relegated.

The pupil at the head of the class stayed there not a minute longer than he (usually "she" in the earlier grades) continued to demonstrate his superiority. Even at a very early age some pupils knew they would never stand at the head of the class. But they left no stone unturned to avoid being left at the foot. In such an environment a great deal of firsthand knowledge was absorbed concerning real-world effort, perseverance, comparisons, compensations, and the general vicissitudes of life.

No quarter was asked, and none was given, among the young competitors. True, there were individuals who were not too bright and who were perhaps unhappy in that sterling environment, but there were no functional illiterates, or illiterates by any other euphemistic designation.

One learned early on how to joust in the marketplace. And this made for a certain degree of introspection and looking to the future; learning to live without a Roman circus or a modern television for diversion.

The Afro-American classroom became untracked at the juncture in history when the tentacles of the "new" education secured their grip on the schools. Succinctly stated, the new education held the emphasis of traditional methods to be misdirected. The ability to reason was to become the objective; memorizing was out. Yet, incredibly, hundreds of whole words were to be learned (not memorized, heaven forbid) instead of the twenty-six-letter alphabet and its associated phonics. Onto the scrap heap went the method whereby any word encountered could be pronounced by synthesizing the sounds of the alphabet of which it consisted.

Once, during the second half of the 1950s, this writer remembers helping a first- or second-grader with his reading lesson. They encountered the word BAT, and the neophyte read right along. When they encountered CAT, he was stumped. This writer was puzzled, but the little boy mollified his tutor by advising that he had studied

BAT but had not yet gotten to the word CAT. He had no inkling of what the letters C-A-T spelled. This was shocking but not really surprising. Within the previous seven or eight years this writer had encountered the first of a series of students registered for college trigonometry who could not extract the square-root of four. The first such student was a freshman girl. These events happened years ago but this writer still remembers the moments when these two youngsters' eyes locked with his. His in horror, and theirs in wonder—at what was bothering him. He remembers the college student's name as well as he does the little boy's. Thinking back over the events, he wonders if they remember. He also wonders what the college student is doing now. She was not stupid, as events proved while they struggled laboriously through the semester, and he hopes she overcame her early educational handicaps. This writer was in a better position to monitor the progress of the bright second-grader. He eventually acquired a remarkable grasp of CAT. In time he became an airline captain, and on misty autumn mornings in the Northeast he shoots CAT II (Instrument Landing System's Category Two) approaches into Logan International Airport.

The new education further mandated that practically every child was a budding genius. The teacher's only job was to encourage the genius to flower. The child would learn at his own rapid speed and the less tutorial interference, the better. Negative reinforcement was considered harmful, positive reinforcement exemplary. Finally, the new education cabal pronounced that henceforth the object of education would be to teach the *child,* not the *subject.*

By this time the great citadels of education (not to be confused with the colleges of liberal arts, engineering, business, etc.) were engaged in deemphasizing teacher- and subject matter-oriented grammar schools, and emphasizing child-centered classrooms instead. The new frontiers of "research" —whose adherents had forgotten Euclid's admonition to King Ptolemy I 2,300 years earlier, "Oh king, there is no royal road to learning," if they ever knew it—sought to extract the work factor from learning and make the acquisition of knowledge *fun.*

Before to the "new" enlightenment, teachers who enjoyed reading and who had an appreciation for words strung skillfully together to conjure up ideas or images were motivated to pass this appreciation on to their pupils. By the same token, any teacher who was fascinated with the interpretation which numbers impart to the relationships between distance, rates, time, and dimensions—not to mention the magical interplay between acceleration, gravity, and curvature—was just as motivated as the reading teacher. As much could be said of the teacher fascinated with faraway places, strange sounding names, and topography, or the one who could breathe life into the exploits and times of Hannibal of Carthage, Attila of the Huns, Runnymede, Christopher Columbus, U. S. Grant, or Sitting Bull.

Before the "great interference," teaching in the Afro-American elementary school was, for the most part, a labor of love. It was a fulfillment of a responsibility the teacher felt for preparing the pupil to cope with a future of expanding opportunities. And the responsibility included a no-nonsense pursuit of passing on the basic skills and knowledge which the pupil would need in the cultural framework of the future. In such an environment teaching was rewarding and singularly effective.

Once the new education decay set in, conditions in the Afro-American elementary classroom deteriorated rapidly. Attempting to conduct C- and J-schools along guidelines laid down for upper-middle-class cultures—where the methods were only marginally successful—was an unmitigated disaster. In homogeneous upper-middle-class communities, parents are aware of the implications of an education and value it enough to put forth the effort to obtain it for themselves and their children. The whole thrust of their lives is toward the future. The direction includes savings, insurance, investments, planning for vacations, and most of all planning for their offsprings' education. The question is never "if" you go to college, but "when" you go to college. Not only does the upper middle class plan for the future, but it also knows how to implement the plans.

On the other hand, in C- and J-culture life is "now" focused: food and drink for today and fun for today. Too many of the refrigerators in the houses of families with young children are filled with beer instead of milk and orange juice. No plans are projected beyond payday or the arrival of the welfare check.

2. J Gets Off to a Bad Start in Education

The first genuine opportunity the pupil from a jive culture has to plug into the mainstream is frittered away by the administration and teachers in his elementary school. J enters school on the first day like a startled deer. His eyes are wide and alert, and his head swivels in every direction. He is ready to strike out along any path which bodes accommodation. This is the moment the teacher should seize to take charge of his life by establishing order, instituting discipline, and laying out guidelines for exemplary work habits and the proper use of time. The pupil will never again be as ready to launch on a course of progressive habits, aspirations, and thought patterns.

Instead of taking the reins of the situation and pressing her natural advantage—which she will have for no more than a few weeks—in order to give the pupil an upward nudge as human instinct and common sense would dictate, the teacher resorts to what the school administration requires and her own courses in education and child psychology dictate. She assumes the posture which she thinks the fledgling student expects of her. She sets about making him feel "at home."

Chances are good that little J is a sloth at home. He runs in the streets and raises hell in the alleys as the mood strikes him. He eats when he is hungry rather than at a regular mealtime, and then only what his own narrow gastronomic experience dictates. Candy and corner store cakes, pies, and potato chips are his choices over vegetables and fruits. His proteins are derived from pork skins, pickled pork feet, and "wings 'n' things" from the corner chicken shack. He prefers carbonated sodas, or maybe even beer, to milk or orange juice. And he tumbles into bed when he is exhausted, and not a moment before. So the very last thing he deserves to have inflicted upon him is to be made to feel "at home." He deserves to be made to feel "in school," where the business at hand is learning and discipline, not indulgence in ignorance, chaos, and sloth.

Professors of education to the contrary notwithstanding, it is a mistake to treat C and J as adults at the age of six years. When a very young child is treated as an adult, he has no incentive to become "big." Commanding the same treatment as the big people, he sees no reason to work for something he has already. People only work for things they desire, and the greater the desire, the greater the effort they are willing to expend.

Before the ascent of the professional educator, in the eyes of the early elementary pupil the principal was big, smart, and obviously in charge of the whole shooting match. The pupil associated size with know-how and authority. In his mind, the three attributes went together, but when the principal (or teacher, as the case may be) spends all his time currying favor, acting servile, trying to be "one of the boys," and—unknowingly—appearing contemptible, as elementary teachers are wont to do in Jivedom, there is no inclination to imitate them. No one wants to emulate an object of scorn. For the most obvious reasons, then, the methodologies worked out in the elementary learning laboratories of the country's most prestigious citadels of education have been singularly unsuited for the Jive elementary school.

The mode of communication that is effective with children from organized, literate, education-oriented homes does not work with children from disorganized, nonliterate, Jive-culture homes. The mainstream pupils are already up to speed when they arrive at elementary school. A systematic approach to the task of learning is merely an extension of their own reality. On the other hand, C and J are strangers to abstractions and conceptualizations. Until they step forward to present themselves for "book learning," their lives have been kaleidoscopes of thoughtless superstitions and frenzies of emotionalism and undirected physical exertion. It is unlikely that they have ever known anyone who was aiming at a goal that was distant though attainable. The people they know are obsessed with gamblers' goals or cultural mirages. Blowing any opportunity he may have to attain his goal is in keeping with the Jive tradition of permitting the trivial or harmful immediacy to eclipse the meaningful objective in the distance. Any teacher worthy of the name knows that the vast majority of beginning pupils must be presented with two alternatives, of which learning is the least painful one. Parental disapproval of unsatisfactory grades, compared to the approval of good ones, is enough to make some pupils attack demanding tasks with vigor. Peer pressure, competition, or both provide sufficient impulse to make other pupils extend themselves until they recognize the relevance of excellence to their own lives. When parental and peer motivation are absent, it

is incumbent upon the teacher to provide effective motivation. Sometimes positive reinforcement will suffice: Sometimes negative reinforcement is required. But *effective* action is essential. Doing nothing is
obscene. The deadly problem in the Jive community elementary school
is that the culture and folkways do not furnish the motivation for
learning, nor do the schools offer up the more unpleasant alternative.

Education is never relevant to C and J when they enter school.
And, unfortunately, it seldom becomes so during their tenure there.
It is the business of the administration and elementary teacher to aim
them in the proper direction until the value of learning becomes obvious
to them. And except for the massive confusion of the theories and
objectives of more than a quarter-century of educational sophistry,
the beginning pupil from the Jive community could be as successfully
taught as the middle-classer.

Once the opportunity to start little C and J on the correct learning
track is miscarried, their whole educational process slushes progressively
down the drain. They soon sense that the entire system is pervaded
with fear and confusion. The teacher is afraid of the principal who
is afraid of the superintendent. The superintendent is afraid of the
board of education whose collective eyes are focused on the city council
and thence to even bigger and better things. The board is not about
to permit the effective education of the progeny of a community of
unconcerned parents to interfere with its own upward mobility.

Most people who have leverage on the learning apparatus are
either afraid or apathetic. The unconcerned teacher presents no problem
to little Jive, and the fearful ones soon become objects to bulldoze.
Before he finishes his second year, school has become more fun than
the playground. Where else can someone intimidate another twice his
size? Instead of being a place of order and industry, the school turns
out to be a nonstop circus. The state of affairs turns reality inside
out. It further augments the basic misconcepts of the Jive community.

By the time J reaches the fifth grade, and from then until he
either quits out of boredom with the charade or graduates, he finds
himself faced with teachers who are trying to be "one of the boys."
No longer are they dressing properly, speaking proper English, or
attempting to exert proper leadership. Most are trying to *relate,* to
even out-youth the youth. The uniforms are faded jeans, jogging shoes

or sneakers, open-collared work shirts, and unkempt beards and hair for the men; and funky, faded hip-huggers, outlandishly trendy hair styles, and silly demeanors reflecting their effort to please everyone for the women.

After six years of schooling it is a point of pride with J that he is not burdened with a knowledge of reading, writing, or health education. And a map of his own city would be as unfathomable to him as the Rosetta Stone.

J leaves grade school with the full knowledge that swaggering through junior high and high school will be even easier than navigating the first six grades has been. Going into the seventh grade as an experienced bully of what is supposed to be authority, he will know exactly how to keep the teachers on the ropes.

Most individuals who could have been effective teachers in Jivedom have long since gone on to less frustrating pursuits. Except for those few diehards within whose hearts hope springs eternal, or for the outright masochists, the majority of the remaining teachers are hopeless, dull, incompetent, or all three. They are cynically putting in time until retirement, awaiting age or disability to relieve them of their miseries, and continuing to fine-hone their expertise in legalizing sloth. They are earning their paychecks (though not for what they are ostensibly being paid), trying to retain what is left of their sanity, and hoping to keep out of physical harm's way.

Once in a long while one hears individuals supposedly concerned with the care and education of the J-juvenile announce banalities regarding education. The proclamation is made that literacy is essential for filing job applications, taking placement tests, and appearing at interviews. Other minimal accomplishments referred to are reading the sports sections of newspapers and traveling locally where street names, the names of different areas of cities, and traffic signs are everyday features of the landscape. The mere mention of these least common denominators of learning, civility, and culture is an ironclad indictment of the low estate of the administration and teaching fabric of Jive education.

There may be something to the old saw that a picture is worth a thousand words. But the idea has qualifications. It does not prevail in the comparison between viewing television and reading for instructive purposes. The obvious advantage of the written word is its duration. Literature which qualifies for the name has been carefully filtered through someone's cognitive processes. The someone may well have been an expert on the subject, and the filtering may have taken place over a period of years. The literature is there to be read repeatedly and, as long as one desires, studied until new insights emerge.

Television productions represent considerable thought and technical *savoir-faire,* but they are created to dazzle. The scenes flash for a few seconds and are gone. They must be quickly assimilated and interpreted, and no more can be absorbed than the viewer brings to the encounter. For basic instructional purposes, the difference between the television and a book is the difference between looking silently at a sheet of music and hearing it interpreted by an accomplished musician.

A downward physical force is more effective than an equal upward one. The difference is especially pronounced when the forces are thrashing about. In education, the gravitational pull toward barbarism is stronger than the buoyancy of culture. Consequently, little J should not be left to learn only when, or if, the spirit moves him. A learning current that sweeps him along should be generated.

3. Early Problems Resulting from Mis-education

The Coping student exerts as little influence on the Jive school as the teachers do. He is accommodating and adaptive while J is aggressively Jive. J is the guiding spirit there, and it is he who establishes the *lingua franca.* And instead of the faculty putting down its collective foot and insisting upon the expression of ideas in standard English, they permit all types of innovative misuse and substitutions for words and parts of speech. One hears an account of the "jive turkey taking stone advantage of the dynamite dude while the latter profiles on the block in his boss threads."

One of the obvious disadvantages of this linguistic aberration occurs at the life and death and bodily injury level. The lack of communication contributes largely to the perennial problem that exists between J and the law enforcement officers assigned to his district. Added to the loathing for authority which his school encourages, J and the policeman use different words, gestures, and facial expressions to transmit the same idea.

Consider what often happens in a crowd-control situation. A policeman wants an individual in the crowd to move back onto the sidewalk and out of the street. He might say, "OK, get out of the street onto the sidewalk. I've told you twice. I'll hit you with this night stick if you don't get back." Here the officer has made a clear statement: what he wants done, how many times he has said so, and what action he will resort to if he is not heeded. Chances are that his statement will not impress J if it is not yelled and accompanied by snarls, scowls, and expletives. J is not familiar with the expression of ideas unembellished with gesticulation. Chances are also that the policeman is unaware of this unfamiliarity, and doesn't have time under the circumstances to give J a chalk talk. In one way or another he thinks he is confronted with defiance of his legal authority. Moreover, chances are that the resulting confrontation will result in an arrest. J will be charged with failure to carry out a legitimate police order. But at his trial he will insist in all sincerity that he was brutalized and arrested "without warning."

Bibliophobes of the type spawned in J's school are denied an essential historical perspective. To talk about "doing one's own thing," except as a joke, is as silly as attempting to reinvent the wheel. Everything one does, says, or thinks takes place within the context of more than six thousand years of history and civilization. There are innovations and reinterpretations of ideas, to be sure, but more important is the art of putting to good use the accumulated experience of humanity.

4. The Product of the J-School

Once out of school, once the bands have quit playing and the teams have retired from the fields and courts, J finds himself physically and emotionally cut loose from his moorings. There are no more math and English teachers to torment, and no more shop and physical education teachers to joust with. There is no place to go when weary of television and the playground.

In some vague, indefinite way J expects to land a job. Having seen people in cars from other sections of the city and the surrounding suburbs pass through his neighborhood during morning and evening rush hours, and seeing people on television going to and from work in cars, he loosely associates cars and other desirable conveniences with work. When he thinks of work he has half-formed expectations of sitting at a desk, answering a telephone, and going out to nice restaurants at lunch time. But what is done at the desk or said over the telephone has never interested him very much. He has no idea of how to acquire one of the jobs he abstractly envisions for himself. Nor does he personally know anyone who holds such a job. But he knows he has to start someplace so he decides on a visit to the employment office.

In his own good time and with his customarily cool demeanor, he drops by the placement agency to see what the world has to offer him. His first impression is that he is entering just another school. People are sitting in rows of chairs in a large room. Other people are sitting at desks facing the audience as his teachers usually did. J harbors no doubt that he is capable of successfully interfacing with this organization. He saunters around the room for a while looking the place over and is mildly annoyed when no one seems impressed with his presence.

When his turn comes for an interview, the response to his swaggering nonchalance is an unconcern bordering on disdain. This is his first inkling that the employment office is not set up to make him feel at home. It is *not* just another school.

But the little shock J sustains at not being able to play the cock of the walk is nothing compared to the jolt of being hit with the battery of application forms, questionnaires, and tests. Suddenly he is as confused as a feral man before a table of integrals.

Once the dust of complete befuddlement settles, J begins to seethe with confused anger. Why is he beset with so many incomprehensibles when he only wants to exercise his God-given right to employment, he wonders. He sees no connection between his desire to earn and the compendium of puzzling papers placed before him.

When he makes his position quite clear to the counselor, he is told with equal clarity that he has to play by the rules of the job-seeking game if he wants to play at all. If he does not, he is as free to leave as he was to enter. But if employment is what he has in mind, his purpose will be best served by sitting himself down and exerting his greatest effort toward filling out the papers.

Thus it happens for the first time. Twelve years behind schedule, the Jive school graduate is faced with a no-nonsense encounter with reality. No one is trying to solicit his love, curry his friendship, or make him feel at home. He is advised what the situation is, what is required of him if he wants to interface with the process, and to make up his mind one way or another; to do the best he can or step aside.

If the Jive school graduate has the presence of mind and adaptability to persevere through what he considers the employment office horror chamber, he may be trajected into one of two slots.

If he is lucky and demonstrates enough desire and promise, he may be directed to one of dozens of available apprentice programs. Given coping inclinations, prospects are good that he will finish the apprenticeship. During the process he will learn at least a smattering of the discipline, habits, and attitudes which he could have learned earlier with greater thoroughness. He could have benefited by them during the twelve years he wasted in school, had he been taught them and had the conduct of the school not been abandoned to Jive.

If he continues to develop, in time J will be able to help his children ascend another rung or two up the socio-economic ladder, rather than look forward to the time when they are "up and out of the way."

A considerable percentage of the students whom circumstances have thrown into Jive's school are not from Jive families. But they become apples in the barrel which the Jive influence spoils. The process does not have to occur, however. And it would not if the school were run as an uncompromising advocate of excellence, and not dedicated to accommodating the least common denominator of conduct and culture. J himself could be redirected. He is not without innate potential, but is a product of culture. He suffers especially from the lack of leadership and the perpetuation of Jivedom's negativisms.

If the Jive school graduate has the luck in the employment which his demeanor usually merits, he will be shunted into a low-paying, dead-end job. Despite his years spent in the proximity of teachers, books, and education pantomime, he will have landed in the stew with the dropouts, the quitters, the incompetents, the maladjusted, and other assorted dodos. And unless he has unusual latent qualities, he will take his place among the members of Jivedom—wrapped as tightly as an orange peel around the bottom rung of the employment ladder.

As the struggle to eke out an existence in subzero weather in winter and in the scorching sun in summer, or in damp, underground holes, dusty bins, or hot laundry rooms continues, J's youthful fantasies will fade in the harsh face of reality, apace with the onset of increasingly intense hostilities and resentments. It is the covert and overt omnidirectional manifestation of their hostilities and resentments which form the central spirit of the Jive community, its moral and intellectual tone, and its general outlook.

Having consciously abandoned the expectation of any improvement in their own lot, the Jive community grows sour and bitter. Its members disdain efforts at self-improvement for themselves and hate it in others. The community is aggressive in its negativism. And having never equated self-betterment with learning, they are xenophobic about the intrusion of mental effort into their lives or their neighborhoods. They miss no opportunity to put down learning, and their dislike for strivers is only matched by their contempt for order and planning.

Part of the J-community ethos is the realization that they lack something desirable which exists in abundance outside their circle. There are so many handles that they see other people using which they are unable to grasp. They vaguely realize that they should have been told something they were not told, shown something they were not shown, and given something they were not given.

Love for their parents precludes them from blaming their families, and their lack of acquaintance with what a school is supposed to accomplish prevents them from laying the onus at the doors of a loathsome educational syndrome. So it is finally something vaguely defined as "the system" which, out of the depths of frustration, they turn on in wrath.

5. J's Rotten-Apple Influence

The very intensity and power of Jive neighborhood malevolence and the authenticity of its core imbues it with radiation power. And like all the diatheses which characterize the community, the malevolence is disabling. It is also infectious. Neighborhoods adjacent to the community—either geographically or through communications—are infected by J's assessment of reality. Some outsiders become spiritual relations through sympathy and some through temperament. Some who look through the one-way screen into Jivedom change their own outlooks. Radiated Jive is especially infectious to outside youth who have adynamic tendencies. And the relatives, friends, and sympathizers of the adynamics often fall into a pattern of identity with the Jive concepts. In time the Jive community inflicts its unhealthy precepts upon the insecure fringe of the larger community in the same way it infects the schools on and within its borders.

When demagogues and opportunists in political clothing sniff out the Jive malady and sympathy in a community, they offer up their nostrums on behalf of its ills. They pretend to know how to stand up to the "system" on behalf of those who have been cheated out of what the "system" owes them. They fan the flames of frustration and resentment so cleverly and diabolically that questions of good government and education are never at issue. All the community's needs are adroitly encapsulated in what the system owes the angry citizens and how, if elected, the opportunist proposes to give the malcontents their due.

Where J is a substantial fraction of the larger community, the opportunist cleverly manages to twist any inquiry concerning efficiency, planning, or public financing to make it sound detrimental to the aspirations of Jivedom.

Now and then an individual with credentials and talent makes a stab at an important elective office. He soon finds out, however, that whenever J represents a substantial block of the electorate, his prospects of winning are inversely proportional to the class and intelligence he exhibits. In fact, the election of a good government is out of the question in a Jive-dominated community.

Candidates for the board of education promise remedial reading courses in high school—never discipline, heaven forbid—while the students in question have just spent the last eight years blowing their chances of learning to read. The truth of the matter is, the typical candidate for the board of education is not remotely interested in quality education. To hear some of them speak makes one doubt their capability even to recognize quality education should they meet its embodiment in the street at high noon.

As for the schools, if someone inside or outside the system suggests a serious pilot program for emendation, the majority of those charged with upgrading education come down on his head with the ire and vituperation reserved for seditionists. They scourge him with such epithets as "betrayer of the heritage," "reviler of the community," and, the ultimate condemnation, "elitist"—the one word most certain to rub raw the nerve that makes J unique. His is the only community anywhere which despises the manifestation of intelligence, prosperity, and class in anyone with whom it identifies.

6. J in College

One of the unfortunate occurrences of the 1960s and early 1970s was the inordinate number of Jive high school graduates who gained entrance into the nation's colleges. They were misfits from the start because acceptance in college is predicated upon excellence, earnestness, a demonstrated desire to develop a talent that society holds in high regard, or all three.

The spirit behind the scholarships and quotas was proper and long overdue. But the method of accomplishing the aim left something to be desired. There were enough Afro-American students who deserved the slots, and who were capable of making good the advantage that a college education offers. Unfortunately, the beneficiaries of these programs seemed to have been selected randomly. And an un-stratified random selection insures as many duds as gems from any population.

Once in college, in juxtaposition with students who had earned their way and whose expenses many of their parents were paying, the Jive high school graduate resorted to the only pattern of conduct he knew. He first tried to bluff and cajole his way. And in what to him was a tractless wasteland, it took him much longer than it took his brother in the employment office to discern that the bluff and cajolery were not working. The business of college education was buzzing all around him. No one was entreating him to study.

No one was pestering him about his assignments or his upcoming essays and term papers. And no one was reacting with either approval or disapproval to his occasional antics. A majority of the other students seemed preoccupied with the class work, and the teacher was moving relentlessly from page to page in the increasingly indecipherable textbook. The entire atmosphere seemed cold, sterile, and impersonal. Instead of the familiar pranking, jousting, loitering, and courting in the corridors, the classrooms were machine-gun nests of rapid-fire lectures, regularly punctuated by wrangles over abstract ideas afloat on mind-blowing words, expressed in unfamiliar thought patterns. Along the hallways, stairways, and walkways between the classrooms, everyone was moving briskly along with some purpose in mind which J was not able to fathom.

In the unfamiliar environment the Jive High alumnus felt isolated. He knew he was lagging behind the pack on the trail. And after having been a part of the leadership in Jive High—one of the pacemakers, in fact—he began for the first time to feel like a failure. His pride required that he do something. He had two choices before him: He could either withdraw from the distressing rat race, or poke around the premises in search of a "soul brother."

Where the setting was a white college, a dissident social group could be assembled under some such sobriquet as the "All-African Rap Group"—a majority of Afro-American students being too busy with their college work to throw in with the separatists. If the setting was a Negro college, the group might have referred to themselves as the "Jocks," the "Jolly Oxen," or the "Anti-Bookworm Brigade." In any case, they often generated enough energy and test-pilfering techniques to hang on with minimum grades and interests all their own.

The bottom rung of the aspiration ladder meant the resentful rung, of course. It meant that Afro-American students higher up the scale were not sources of inspiration but objects of envy and derision. And in the same way that the inhabitants of the Jive community who are viewed through one-way windowpanes evoke sympathy for their deprivation and envy for their easy, unstructured lifestyle, many of their college mates empathized with the dissidents. Occasionally significant segments of the student body were infected.

The tip of the iceberg of the Jive students' influence was seen again and again. At one time, student strikes threatened colleges accused of providing unsatisfactory meals in the dining hall or enforcing overly strict rules of conduct. At other times grumblings and rumblings arose over the requirements of unrealistically high academic standards.

Why would the complainants remain at institutions they found so abominable? Their protest was another manifestation of the Jive mentality. They wanted to slow the pace of the project to zero, to dilute the rules of the game to chaos but receive a prize for being on location. Or more specifically, the complainants wanted to slouch through four years of college, yet receive diplomas to parade before the world.

A definitive example of Jive influence at a university happened a few years ago when a gaggle of law school graduates raised a ruckus about the difficulty of the bar examination. Apparently a number of them had failed it. Of course, they said, it was not their fault. According to their spokesman, the crystal-clear, obvious reason for the outcome was racism. Not that the examination given Afro-Americans was *different* from that given whites, but that it was the *same*. It had a mainstream American, rather than a black, cultural slant. Imagine, an opportunity to go to a modern school and study in a modern library, an opportunity to hear distinguished and inspiring lecturers, and finally, an opportunity to take the examination. And what was the reaction to this wealth of opportunity? An enraged scream of "foul." Where would the Afro-American be now if Charles Houston, James Nabrit, and Thurgood Marshall had spent their youths whimpering about the inscrutability of American jurisprudence?

These screams of outrage from some of the future Negro lawyers of America were made self-righteously. The students truly believed that they should have been given a different bar examination, one slanted more toward Afro-American culture than mainline American culture.

One wonders what the complainants had in mind. Did they propose to represent Afro-American clients only? If so, how did they plan to represent them in mainstream courts against mainstream attorneys without a grasp of mainstream jurisprudence? Finally, how much clamor would these lawyers raise if, having entered the profession by way of a special minority examination, they decided to switch to corporate or government law, and no firm or agency would touch them?

To add insult to ignominy, many of these young protesters went into what, for the lack of a better name, is referred to as "the black leadership pool." They had modern credentials. Having begun their protest careers in college, they were following in the footsteps of some of their more sensational predecessors. And since the serious Afro-American student is inspired by the possibilities of expanding opportunity in business, economics, engineering, the natural sciences, and, yes, the law, the leadership pool is dominated by the professional protesters. It is they who will return to lead C and J to the Promised Land. And given their Jive viewpoint and sympathies, and the direction in which they are launching their careers, there is little question that they will continue the style of "leadership" that has hung like a millstone around C's and J's necks for the last two decades.

The latter-day leaders have hewed to the line that all the trouble and problems of the Jive community are color-based, that the establishment interacts with the disadvantaged on a strict white/black basis. Although many variables may influence an encounter, variables other than color become blurred and meaningless for them. In the absence of color considerations, individuals may be chosen or rejected for companionship or employment, to name two examples, on the basis of intelligence, personality, neatness, height, weight, wealth, ability, nationality, or even religion. But where color is involved, all other factors are eclipsed, they claim, and any disability J suffers is inflicted by the system.

The schools are inadequate because too little money is appropriated, the latter-day leaders contend. The alleys are filthy because the city does not clean them regularly in Jivedom. Drugs abound because the law enforcement apparatus is not exercised in J's interest. Crime is high because the police force is corrupt. Jobs are scarce because the stores, factories, and offices have deserted the center city for the suburbs. Smaller stores in Jivedom will not cash checks because the system does not trust the inhabitants. And on and on the litany goes.

The point that the schools may be poor because the vast majority of the students are more inclined to disruption than study, thus robbing the classrooms of a learning atmosphere, is never considered. The suggestion that the alleys would not be filthy if bottles, cans, paper, and chicken bones were not regularly strewn in every direction is never made. The proposition that drugs would disappear from the neighborhood if the neighbors set goals for themselves other than a hedonistic desire for a temporary "high" is never explored. By the same token, the cause of crime as a result of one's neighbors' effort to best another by foul means is never pointed out.

As for jobs, the most obvious fact in the world—that J is unsuited in training, habits, and outlook for most modern jobs—is never uttered. And the fact that the small stores and shops are correct when they think a majority of the citizens trading in the vicinity consider it clever to "get over" with a rubber check is overlooked.

J's leadership pulls out all the stops to augment his belief that he is history's victim—a victim of racism, the system, and a nefarious plan to cheat him of whatever civilization owes him. J is encouraged to maintain his victim psychology, and nothing is mentioned of what he owes himself.

That an abundance of choice food, clothing, housing, automobiles, bicycles, and, yes, jobs, exists is indisputable. Anyone can get a glimpse into the national cornucopia any night of the week via his or her television. And the modern leadership addresses itself to *what* material blessings their clientele should have, but not *how* the blessings were acquired by those who have them. They tell J what they think he *wants* to hear rather than what they know, or should know, that he *needs* to hear. The subjects of study, work, discipline, order, perseverance, responsibility, reliability, and honesty are never touched upon.

7. J's Needs

The Coping and Jive citizens need hands-on care: They need directions that reach into their lives of chaos, confusion, and drift to stabilize and direct their abundant energies. A fledgling student pilot receives hands-on instruction, for example. It is called follow-me-through on the controls. Without it, all concerned would take much longer to learn the art, and some would never learn. In a first attempt to execute a turn the airplane rolls, yaws, pitches, skids, and bounces simultaneously. The cockpit is a confusing cage as lethal as an electric chair—authenticated by the arresting shoulder straps and safety belt. The student has studied his manual and performed the feat in his mind a hundred times. He knows what he wants to do, but the feel for the maneuver is not there. The world is reeling and twisting, and the wind is alternately whistling and swishing.

Then the instructor advises, "Follow-me-through on this turn." After a few follow-throughs the miracle occurs. The rogue aircraft seems to come to a smooth standstill. It sits docilely in mid-air while the world turns slowly, evenly, and calmly below. For the first time the student sees the light at the end of the tunnel; really believes that eventually he will become a pilot. He is suddenly in a new dimension of enthusiasm and hope. His whole state of mind, his resolve and confidence are the result of caring, hands-on instruction at an early stage in the game.

By contrast, neither the grand pronouncement from the mountain-top, the ego trip across the television screen, nor the combative news conference touches the youth submerged in the Jive community. Situated as he is behind the one-way viewing screen, the words from on high have no relevance to J's life. They are articulated by people who he thinks "have it made" in an area which is strange and foreign to him.

The speech from the mountain should be directed to an inter-mediary, to someone who understands the message well enough to act out the directions on a personal level with J. The times cry out for a national leader who understands what the typical youth afloat in the Jive community needs and who understands how to address these needs in specifics.

All the freedom, opportunity, and Head-Start programs in the United States will not alleviate J's condition until a leader arises on the horizon who has presence, charisma, conviction, and courage. In no uncertain terms, this leader will call for study, order, and industry; study, training, and education; study, planning, and thrift; and study, control, and self-reliance. He will advocate an enthusiasm for living, progress, and mainstreaming. His message will be entirely upbeat. It is out of the frame of mind created in this way that "black pride" will come—rather than from the mimicry of some millionaire ignoramus, screaming at the top of his pot-powered lungs and gyrating his head and hips to a barbaric drumbeat.

Marva Collins is a teacher in Chicago who had all she could stomach of the traditional ghetto schools, so she started her own. In her living room at home she began a series of no-frills classes in reading, writing, arithmetic, and literature. She was a natural teacher whose subject matter was dear to her heart. She felt a compulsion to pass it on to young minds.

The fortunate children under her influence began learning subjects which their communities had previously considered complicated and irrelevant. They learned at a rate of speed which the "educators" erroneously considered amazing. Mrs. Collins knew what she wanted and how to go about producing it. She brought the teaching artist's enthusiasm to her classroom, and the students got into the spirit of the activity immediately.

Mrs. Collins' venture had notable advantages over the traditional Jive community school. She had no superintendent and principal, with their gaggle of assistants, looking over her shoulder to see that she kept the faith with modern elementary education orthodoxy. She had no board of education whose squabbling, posturing members' primary objective was moving up the next rung of the political ladder. Thus, she had no pressure to tolerate the streetwise bully, who was diabolic enough to use the aims, objectives, and theories of the school administration and the crassness of the board to turn her classrooms into confrontation carousels. Her classrooms had order, purpose, and were teacher-centered.

The requisite courage to undertake an expedition through the exasperating mine field of present-day education in the Afro-American community is extremely rare. But such an exemplary idea occurs occasionally—and not always as a metropolitan phenomenon. A truly innovative program has been under way for the past three years in tiny Anniston and its environs in central-eastern Alabama. An organization called Education Par Excellence, the brainchild of a minister named John R. Nettles, is in the process of revising the climate of apathy and rejectionism which more often than not envelopes predominantly Afro-American elementary and secondary schools.

Education Par Excellence has devised a strategy to create a community ethos of cooperation and approval to replace the *onus pobandi* or even hostility which any perceptible intellectual exertion customarily encounters. The tactics include academic pep rallies in school auditoriums when the occasion is intramural and in stadiums when the activity is interscholastic. They also include declaring certain evening hours to be study periods by having them announced over the radio stations to which the students listen and dispatching roving squads to see if the students are studying. Those in compliance are given awards and public recognition. And increasingly, within the radius of Education Par Excellence's activity, academic excellence is becoming "cool" rather than "square."

There are individuals all across the country who have the makings of inspired teachers. They are fascinated with an assortment of branches of knowledge and would like to impart them to young minds. Some are presently in teaching positions and are not permitted to teach. And there are those who have been teachers, who threw up their hands in disgust, pronouncing a plague on the houses of both the administrations and the student types created by the education system.

Under the aegis of a prestigious national leader who perseveres in a campaign for study, planning, and discipline, until the idea attracts the Jive community's attention, the aspiring teachers could take their places in the front ranks of education there. No longer would they have to either quit the scene or cower on the fringes of the carnival.

8. Posturing for J

Every middle-class parent is intimately acquainted with the importance of start-up skills. A child needs to be shown such basic skills as how to use a spoon, knife, fork, toothbrush, and comb, how to sit at the dinner table, and how to say "thank you." And in school he has to be shown how to hold a pencil. The absence of the most basic start-up skills defines the difference between the middle-class child and J—often referred to as the deprived child, and called "lower class" in a less egalitarian age.

There are many definitions of a middle-class parent. But the most definitive one describes the parent who is able to do something for the offspring in a timely manner which the offspring could not do for itself. If not shown how to use a spoon, a child would eat with his fingers. And given a spoon without instructions on its use, he would eventually stumble onto some technique for employing it. The child could "get by" with this fortuitous find, but the technique would hardly be as socially acceptable or functional as long years of civilization would dictate.

An especially sensitive, observant, industrious child would eventually learn the proper use of the spoon and toothbrush and how to say "thank you," and would maybe even work his or her way through trade school or college without middle-class parenting. But the efforts would take considerably more time, require much more work, and leave permanent personality scars, which are not left on children whose middle-class parents provide decreasing but positive hands-on aid through the transition from infancy to adulthood. Children without such parents, and who would not be especially observant, sensitive, and industrious if not for outside intervention, grow up to be deprived adults.

Children are proud of their parents who have made headway against unlikely odds and gained ground not given to the frivolous. And parents are even more proud of their children who accomplish objectives which mere living, breathing, and demanding would not warrant. In the same way, ethnic pride is based on accomplishment. It derives from a deed resulting from more than mere being, but from being something significant.

The tragic truth is that J is a creation of his spokesmen. Prior to the 1960s he was half-apologetic for his sloth and felt he should have been doing better by himself, doing more with his life. But, after digesting the message of his latter-day prolocutors, he became self-righteous in "doing his own thing."

In addition to the envy of its carefree lifestyle and the empathy for its blues interpretation of history, the Jive community manages to transmit a third infliction through the one-way screen to the surrounding environment. An insidous guilt and embarrassment at their own accomplishments cling like leeches to the skins of many of the talented Afro-Americans who have at one time or another brushed against the ideas emanating through the Jive filter screen.

An example of this phenomenon is the encounter that took place a few years ago between two Afro-American scientists and a community of bush blacks in the jungles of South America. The scientists were from one of the most prestigious universities in the country. The community of blacks consisted of the progeny of slaves brought to Dutch Guiana who had escaped into the impenetrable rain forest. There, for more than a quarter of a millennium they had symbiosed, on bitter roots, with the piranha and fer-de-lance under conditions worse than those from which they had been uprooted in Africa. They improved neither their style of living nor frame of mind over the centuries. But they had developed a hardscrabble pride in not having submitted to slavery and a toughness which had permitted them to survive under such adverse conditions.

These bush men must have had, at one time or another, at least some semblance of contact with the outside world. According to the account of their encounter with the scientists, as soon as communications were established, the village elders posed a series of patronizing questions to which they wanted straight answers.

They wanted to know the purpose of the scientists' visit, if they had ever gotten their freedom from slavery in the United States, and if they were going to be permitted to return home—to Africa—yet.

The queries were not surprising, coming as they did from a people suspended in a primeval time warp since the 1600s. The surprise was the scientists' account of having stood shamefaced before the regal inquisitors. Regal? What had they accomplished except a static survival barely above the animal level for more than three centuries? They had neither relocated nor improved their local environment enough to provide the leisure necessary to invent a wheel, an hourglass, or a candle—not to mention such basic civilizing implements as books, clocks, and incandescent light bulbs.

Another example involves a famous author who trekked to visit an African tribe. He said, among other things, when he returned, that he stood humbled, surrounded by the pure blackness he encountered there.

A number of obvious questions come to mind concerning the reaction of these three gentlemen. Were they telling the truth? If so, why did they, all accomplished individuals measured by the technological world's standard of excellence, feel inadequate and humbled before a group of people whose only accomplishment was being? And if they thought they had found a purist paradise, why did they not remain on the respective southern continents and soak up those timeless virtues for the remainder of their lives? True, the mainstream world may have been the poorer for their having secluded themselves in the jungles, but one suspects that the world might have survived their absence.

To ask another question: Were these accomplished Afro-Americans fabricating what they thought they were expected to say, or saying what they thought they were supposed to feel? Finally, were they playing to the Jive community and its spokesmen? If so, why did they think they had to do so? If, in fact, they were posturing for J and his spokesmen, then J has more influence on them than they have on him. It should be the other way around. They should have long since outgrown the reach of Jive-inflicted cultural schizophrenia.

Both Americans and foreigners of any hue and hyphenation living here waiting to become citizens make pilgrimages back to their points of origin every year. They visit Europe, Africa, Latin America, and the Far and Near East. They stand before hovels and substantial houses, on steppes, savannas, and wind-swept seashores. But they never report having stood humbled before their kith and kin who, for one reason or another, stayed put. The travelers all seem unabashedly glad they landed where they did. So the question arises again: Why were these three men embarrassed with their U.S. passports tucked safely in their pockets?

If J's present leadership ever gave their unapologetic blessings and advocacy to individual and group training and education, self-improvement, self-discipline, and self-reliance, there would be no need to apologize for accomplishment. But of course there would be no need of their leadership either, based upon promises of acquiring grants and community development funds, of standing up to the establishment, and, of course, of strangling in the cradle any idea surfacing in the community on which the tag "elitist" could be pinned—whether it be a chess club, an actors' guild, or a designated academic school.

9. The Stage is Set for a Leader

To observe the obvious, innumerable talented and accomplished individuals have risen out of the Afro-American community in a steady stream since the 1700s. Afro-Americans have made signal contributions to progress in the United States since Benjamin Banneker, the astronomer-mathematician-clockmaker, who was among the first Americans to accurately predict a solar eclipse, and who was appointed by President Washington to the commission that drew up the city plans for the Nation's capital. Afro-Americans have made contributions in mechanical inventions, literature, scholarship, medicine, art, history, science, music, the performing arts, education, the military, and law. Thurgood Marshall, for example, made a significant contribution in the latter. He was a product of and one of the contributors to the important civil rights jurisprudence developed by law deans, professors, and students at Howard University in the 1940s and early 1950s.

The sneers of "gradualism" from the post-1965 spokesmen to the contrary notwithstanding, the legal philosophy and its successful execution, with Marshall as the point man, left its mark on American history for all time.

By all accounts, the strategy that led to the series of Supreme Court victories was prefaced by extremely demanding law courses, long and exacting research, and interminable mock trials lasting through endless overlapping days and nights. On one side were the plaintiffs, and on the other a battery of devil's advocates who played the role from years of bitter personal court experiences. The devil's advocates tried every ruse imaginable to justify keeping King James Crow on the throne.

As a result of this brand of preparation, Marshall was able to penetrate any defense of Jim Crowism, on sound legal grounds, that its defenders threw up. He and his associates gave the country and the world a new and poignant interpretation of social injustices, which for hundreds of years had been romanticized as benevolent, realistic, and proper. And the rulings in some of the thirty-odd cases he argued before the Supreme Court will be quoted as precedent as long as social conflict survives in the English-speaking world and beyond.

One of the more significant qualities of the self-images of both Banneker and Marshall, and the legions of talented Afro-Americans who came in-between, is that they did not view themselves as leaders. They would have been abashed at the thought. They went about their callings in a thoroughly workmanlike manner. Few of them ever mused over whether they were constructing stone walls or cathedrals.

Afro-Americans of Banneker-Marshall caliber, like accomplished individuals of any race, caste, or class, were creatures of aspiration, preparation, and perspiration. They aimed high, prepared carefully, and worked tirelessly to attain their goals. They spent no time looking for shortcuts, expecting lucky breaks, or hoping for gifts or grants. On the rare occasions when they unearthed serendipitous advantages, they took them in stride with the full knowledge that the lucky hand is the skillful hand, nine times out of nine. Their lives characterized none of the selfishness and frivolity of purpose prevalent in the post-1960s spokesmen.

The facilities for communication and the depth of education and experience in the Afro-American community of the 1980s are such that Washington's type of educational leadership could be mounted without someone of Washington's range of talents. There are enough people of Marva Collins's persuasion who are willing, able, and eager to move to give the Jive community a permanent facelift. Lacking, however, is a charismatic focal point around which the teaching artists can rally. A long-standing need exists for someone who has the capability to capture J's imagination, but who will not tremble and retreat in the teeth of the storm that is sure to arise when he first announces that there is no "free lunch." One must pay, always—if not in currency or honest work, then in violated self-esteem.

This leader must be willing to give the benefit of his knowledge, education, and experience to the community rather than use the community as a constituency for his political and financial ambitions. He must not back down before the boisterous youth and try to become "one of the boys" by imitating their dress, language, and thought patterns. He must stand his ground and repeat his message over and over until the refrain is triggered in the minds of his constituency from a variety of cues taken from everyday experience, like the words of a familiar song.

The leader would not have to possess the world's greatest talent for hands-on instruction. His role would consist of establishing a psychological framework in which hands-on talent could work. The framework would diminish the negative community sentiment that has neutralized useful talent for the last quarter of a century.

Chapter 5

AFRO-AMERICAN LEADERSHIP: RELIGION AND SOCIAL MORALITY

1. The Storefront Church

If the efficacy of leadership is judged by the cultural enlightenment and material well-being it imparts to its constituency, the Afro-American religious variety to which C and J are exposed has been a dismal failure. Its purpose has remained invariant since the eighteenth-century bondsmen regularly stole away into the groves and assembled around upside-down kettles. They believed that the inverted utensils muffled their orgies of singing, shouting, testifying, and lamentation. Their rituals served as vehicles of escape from "this vale of tears" to a few minutes of the spiritual ecstasy that their religion promised would be the eternal reward of the faithful.

Most churches in and adjacent to the Jive community are of the storefront variety. They steadily replace the businesses that disappear from the scene. Small entrepreneurs flee when the substantial spenders who justify their existence move away, when an expanded shopping center locates within a convenient distance, or when thieves, muggers, and vandals become sufficiently aggressive to turn small ventures into losing propositions. As these establishments cede the territory, preachers in search of places to locate or relocate their flocks splash a bit of cheap paint and crudely drawn crosses on the windows of the buildings and move in.

There are always Jive preachers on the prowl for locations. Some begin with curbstone services and decide to move indoors after accumulating a dozen or so regular followers. Others lead splinter groups of procedural dissenters from ongoing flocks. And still others deliberately stir up dissension and splinter congregations in which they belong once it occurs to them that a gold mine and an ego trip accompanies having flocks of their very own. What could be more rewarding to a shrewd, half-illiterate egomaniac than a few dozen followers worshiping according to his interpretation of the Holy Writ, and, in addition, tithing for the privilege of being dictated to?

The yokel always has an automobile the length of his church front because he always has a building or renovation program in progress—new pews, kitchens, carpeting, or stained glass—and somehow, in the process, the Lord always "blesses" him with a Cadillac, a Chrysler, or a Lincoln. Since he is God's messenger, or instrument, or whatever, why shouldn't he cruise in heavenly opulence while the more fortunate members of his flock of tithers rattle along in vehicles with retread tires and dragging tailpipes? The less fortunate convey their tithe by public transportation, thankful to be blessed with enough money left beyond their "religious obligations" to afford round-trip bus fare.

2. The Storefront Church Mentality

Churches of the storefront genre could never be uprooted from their environment—nor should they be. With their shouting, testifying, unknown-tongue talking, and foot-washing rituals, they serve a purpose for their membership that transcends anything to be derived from analysis, ratiocination, or even plain horse sense. If, by some queer legal happenstance, laws were enacted to abolish them, the event would only serve to strengthen their influence. It would offer up an opportunity for martyrdom with which a "freedom of religion" country has only a biblical acquaintance. Such an event would herald in the brand of clean, pristine faith that none but the righteous who expect to be caught up in the "rapture" are capable of experiencing.

To say that the storefront churches should not be eradicated does not imply that they should not evolve. They remain forever as primitive as the original inverted-pot gatherings only because of the types of individuals who occupy their pulpits. The flocks have implicit faith in their leaders. The shepherd has his worshippers convinced that he has been chosen by God to interpret the sacred law and guide the faithful along the path of salvation. The measure of his control of their minds is shown by their willingness to render a tenth of their inadequate earnings to God through the pastor's hands without an accounting.

For the most part, the storefront lambs are individuals whom the complexities of urban life have left in shock. From their fetal positions they do not associate their leaders' comparative wealth with their tithes. Many among them are literal flat-earthers. Their authority is the biblical passage referring to the four corners of the world.

The preacher justifies his conduct because it serves the flock at the level of their needs. He convinces himself that the nature of their problems and cultural shackles is so complex that a holding operation is better than tampering with something that could boil over into a disaster.

The abiding thrust of the little church is escapism. Life is not conceived as a set of circumstances and challenges to be considered, analyzed, and come to terms with. It is an incomparable plot of sin, temptation, and unmitigated evil; something from which the righteous should withdraw. Unfortunate circumstances have put the faithful "in the world," but they are not "of the world." The singular purpose of life is to strengthen one's resolve to "yield not to temptation" in preparation for eternal bliss—where there will be no crushing conundrums, no trials and tribulations, and "no dark valleys."

One's earthly obligations consist of nothing beyond tithing and bearing up. To this end, storefront religion is profoundly negative-supportive, a sacred version of the blues. The outstanding feature of the regularly held testifying ritual is its inevitable downward spiral. Each testimony reveals greater trials, temptations, and suffering than the preceding one. Those who bare their souls first are made to feel thankful. No matter what they had thought upon arriving at the meeting, their burdens are lighter than those of their brothers and sisters who testify later. The entropy continues unabated until the flock can endure the mounting agony no longer, and the spirit descends upon them in an orgy of screaming, shouting release.

3. Opportunities Unheeded As Usual

A measure of the microcaliber of the storefront leadership is that nothing under its care and tutelage increases except its own coffers and the size of the buildings it occupies. With the extraordinary influence it exerts over its assembly, terrestrial miracles could be wrought. Yet all the opportunities for earthly advancement have been passed up throughout Afro-American history.

These churches could organize credit unions. No greater good could be rendered a little affinity group than having the members band together to lend one another financial aid in times of adversity. The members could be shown the value of nursing a nest egg for a rainy day and, at the same time, observing its growth through investment. In short, the church members could be imbued with habits of self-help, mutual aid, and money management. But what advice are they given in this area? "Lay not up for yourself treasures on earth where moths and dust doth corrupt and thieves break in and steal." And the flock mentality is such that it does not bother them that their spiritual advisor is doing precisely the contrary.

An apartment building could be purchased. At any given moment, at least two or three members of the little band are apartment-, efficiency-, or room-hunting. Poised precariously on either side of poverty's boundary line, as a substantial number of them are, their housing is sometimes substandard and often on a month-to-month basis. Those whose abodes are rented rooms are usually out of the weather on nothing more substantial than verbal contracts of a week's duration. What then could better serve the welfare, well-being, and peace of mind of the flock than a cooperative investment in an apartment building—under the auspices of a spiritual leader whom they trust and from whom they are willing to learn.

A food co-op could be organized. This might require a bit more start-up expertise than a credit union or an apartment co-op. Handling perishables requires faster footwork and sterner immediacies than carrying a member's money to the bank or keeping his or her living quarters in good repair. But the hurdle could be overcome by the same persistent cleverness that builds a zero-based curbstone membership into a thriving, tithing, growing, fifty-to-a-hundred-member chapel. That such a venture would be of value to the membership is without question. There would be jobs in the offing, techniques of business management to be learned, and, not the least of considerations, cheaper food for people on the marginal incomes on which many of such flocks exist.

In addition to jobs, training, and bargain food, other obvious blessings would accrue. The members would be brought closer together by working shoulder to shoulder on an uplifting enterprise. The project could become an extension of their worship services, and the shepherd could extend his influence into yet another dimension of their lives.

The little flocks could be led into restaurant businesses, catering ventures, janitorial services, dry cleaning establishments, and a host of other community enterprises. And from these vantage points of high public visibility, they could set lofty ethical standards and exert a good influence in their neighborhoods rather than shrugging off the world as a sin-ridden loss.

Of course, there is always the risk that too much earthly security would undermine someone's dependence upon the fellowship that clinging to the flock provides. And in the process of acquiring worldly goods and focusing a bit on their advantages and management, some of the members—other than the quota of new preachers who are "called" out of all flocks to organize one of their own—might also become independent and disobedient. Apparently, storefront religious leadership chooses to avoid such risks to exchequer and ego.

4. The Shortchanged Flock

Apparently, less than one in a thousand of the storefront poobahs throughout Afro-American history ever thought of leading his membership into mutual self-help enterprises, or, if the thought occurred, the know-how was missing. But with precious few exceptions, events bear out the even stronger possibility that such leaders are in the advice-dispensing business for the spiritual uplift of their flocks and their own material uplift.

One suspects that temporal viability is out of character with the very nature of storefront religious philosophy. Its very cornerstone is laid upon the assertion that individuals are helpless vis-à-vis the corruption and complexities of human society. That mankind is essentially evil and depraved. And that the individual's only salvation lies in drawing away from society's hell-bent influence. Society's methods, aims, and objectives are wrought by the devil, and only Grace, as dispensed by whatever chapel to which one happens to belong, is capable of saving one from everlasting torment.

And since the normal social processes have dealt so harshly with most of the members of the flock, according to the storefront inter-pretation of their plight, another trip through hell is more than they care to chance. Getting ahead in this world, or even holding one's own through the exercise of one's energy, initiative, and plans holds no apparent attraction. And it turns out that everyone, shepherd and flock alike, is as pleased as punch with the status quo. The pastor manages to keep the flock's eyes focused on the distant hereafter while he jostles them about their moral shortcomings in the present and systematically picks their pockets.

Unfortunately, it is usually to the religious exemplars and mysta-gogues rather than the secular successful that Jive's aspiring spokesmen look for cues. The reasons are many—not the least of which is the shallow nature of the aspirants.

The religious grandees are always accorded more adulation, loyalty, and financial support than their worth to the community justifies. Their ascent to influence results from the clever way they play on the harp of superstition and ineptitude of the souls who are disposed to listen to them.

The storefront charmer usually has about him the aura of the sorcerer rather than the sophrosyne (the quality of stability and good judgment) of a man with a plan. He proposes to put projects on track through faith, and to escape mundane problems through magical projections into an extraterrestrial future.

5. J's Secular Spokesmen Imitate his Religious Mentors

The bedrock of an intense religion is a community of adherents with an abiding impression of their own impotence. Each individual must perceive himself ensnared in grievous circumstances from which escape is beyond his or her physical powers or mental acuity. This psychophysical environment is then ripe for a seer who brings along a demonology and the hope of escape through ritual and faith.

Taking a page from the storefront religious leader's notebook, J's aspiring spokesman conjures up a secular demonology. It goes under a multiplicity of monikers including "the man," "the system," "society," "poverty," or "exploitation." Having come out of Negro folkways and having thus been graced with considerable validity, the demonology has a long history. It also has the potential for serving no purpose beyond the aims of the schemer who employs it. Like the proverbial straw man, it is repeatedly set up and knocked over long after the conditions which justified its use have passed into history.

The fledgling spokesmen of the post-sixties era quote from the same negativist scripture that the traditional storefront church leader uses. The expressions are regularly permuted to confuse the issue, but the sum and substance of the message is the same: "Within the clutches of the circumstances where we find ourselves, we are helpless—except for the magic formula which has been revealed to me. Do not burden your minds attempting to decipher these puzzles of evil and chicanery. Just follow me. I will lead you to the relief and salvation you deserve."

No admonition is issued in the interest of attempting to understand the forces which swirl around one's head; to make a thoughtful adjustment to the gusts, which, if properly employed, may serve as tail winds rather than head winds or crosscurrents. The message is always razzle-dazzle rather than ratiocination, and it is always about what is *deserved* through mere existence rather than what may be *earned* through planning and concentration.

6. Storefront Christianity's Narrow Concerns

The religion that circumscribes C and J is no more life-and-welfare affirming than their schools or the other activities indigenous to the community. The churches subscribe to the same format as mainline religious institutions, but their emphasis is on the preparation for death. Their moral concerns are strictly personal. Extramarital sex is forbidden, for example. It is a pleasure (God forbid) of the flesh, a carnality which detracts from the purity of the soul to its eternal damnation. Broader concerns, such as precautions against veneral diseases or the prevention of having children out of wedlock, do not factor into the prohibition.

A religion insensitive to the health and legitimacy of its own membership could hardly be expected to concern itself with a different ethnic group in the way the little band of Rhode Island Quakers did in 1652. By then transplanted to the American colonies, the Quakers broadened their concerns about religious rites and procedures to include a protest against human slavery. They made their anti-slavery position so clear, with such fervor, that they eventually inspired the concern of the other Quaker groups in the Northeast. It became a part of their protocol.

Elizabeth Griscom's name appeared on the roll of the Phildelphia Friends' Meeting in the last third of the 1700s. At the age of twenty-one Elizabeth eloped with John Ross. It is not hard to imagine Betsy Ross, the seamstress, the maker of the first United States flag, spending moments of silent meditation on behalf of Negro manumission as well as on the salvation of her own soul.

Protestant concern has included the secular as well as the spiritual well-being of humanity since the Reformation in the 1500s. The institutional concern has been reflected in the individual concern of a countless number of its adherents. And concern with the welfare of someone other than oneself is the definition of sympathy. Harriet Beecher Stowe, daughter of Congregational minister Lyman Beecher, was concerned with the plight of the Negro slave when she wrote *Uncle Tom's Cabin.*

Nearly a century after the publication of *Uncle Tom* and a half-continent away from Mrs. Stowe's New England, James Farmer became interested in implementing the constitutional rights of Afro-Americans. An Afro-American himself and a seminary student, Farmer's interpretation of religious studies pointed to humanity's earthly well-being as a first priority.

In 1947 Farmer embarked on a "freedom ride" with an integrated group of participants sponsored by the Fellowship of Reconciliation. A year earlier the Supreme Court had ruled that the diversity of racial regulations applying to interstate carriers in different states imposed an unreasonable hardship on travelers. The freedom ride was designed to test whether certain states along the northern tier of the Confederacy were complying with the spirit of the Court's ruling.

Fourteen years later in 1961, as the national director of the Congress of Racial Equality (CORE), Farmer organized and led his more famous "freedom ride." The ride consisted of a bus trip from Washington, D.C., to New Orleans. The participants included Farmer—who went at the head of the group as military leaders did before military leadership became an executive plum—and six Negroes and six whites.

From his ministerial training and from various groups to which he had belonged, Farmer had developed a "non-violent direct action" philosophy. It provided for the protestation of social injustice by presenting one's body in sacrifice to evil. The sacrifice was to be made in love, compassion, and understanding, without physical resistance. The philosophy assumed that whatever violence resulted from the presentation resulted from ignorance rather than malevolence; and that its perpetrators would in time sicken at the sight of the blood they drew and the bruises they inflicted,that they would eventually withdraw from the fray to a higher moral plane newly discovered within themselves. There was always the possibility that evil's enlightenment would come too late for any given sacrificially minded individual, but it would be beneficial to the cause. The possibility of self-sacrifice was the risk dictated by the moral crusade.

Additional freedom rides were organized in the wake of the 1961 journey. By the time they ended a month later, every eventuality Farmer had foreseen had come to pass. Free citizens attempting to exercise their rudimentary constitutional rights had been confronted and attacked across the entire southeastern quadrant of the country. The despicable brouhaha had drawn worldwide attention and the intervention of the federal government on behalf of Negro civil rights.

Martin Luther King, Jr. represents the most prominent example in recent years of a theologian whose training suggested the need for action in the temporal arena. Although his name is invoked universally and often, J's religious leadership seems oblivious of the association between Dr. King's ministry and the concerns he had with humanity's social and economic welfare. These ministers give

King's endeavors lip service but keep their own narrow agendas focused on the hereafter and the collection plate.

King's trials with the Improvement Association in Montgomery, his tribulations in Birmingham and Selma, and his triumphant March on Washington are nationally recounted at least once per year when his birthday is celebrated. But mainstream Protestantism as an example aside, his aspirations sketched a new dimension to black folk-religion. He saw the Afro-American experience in a Euclidean spirituality in which both the problems and the solutions existed in a common terrestrial plane—in direct contrast to the moth-eaten orthodoxy which proclaimed celestial eurekas.

7. J's Need for Wider Concerns

Considering the stakes that the church leaders in J's community have in one-dimensional religion, it is unlikely that any of them will tamper with the present machinery. If the needed change ever occurs it will arrive as the result of outside intervention. It will not be effected by generalized hints made from afar nor, obviously, by a remote example. King's *modus operandi* was clear enough had J been susceptible to an example unaccompanied by specific and detailed instruction.

The intervention must be made by a leader with national authority, and the message should be addressed primarily to J's religious leaders. The national leader must have a clear understanding of what is needed as well as enough prestige to create an ideological force field in which local leaders would realize that ignoring the message would be done at their peril.

A genuine two-dimensional spirituality would release magical sources of energy in the J-community. A conviction that an education or setting aside a nest egg, for example, had religious countenance would constitute a phenomenal buoy on a street where ambition is so futile that ridicule seems the proper attitude toward it. Undreamed-of avenues of self-improvement would be discovered and set out upon. And Dr. King's endeavor, now unclearly understood, could be seen in clear focus and in the true two-dimensional context in which it was forged.

Some of history's most significant exploits have been religiously motivated or done in the name of religion. The wildfire spread of Islam in the sixth and seventh centuries and the Christian Crusades between 1095 and 1272 immediately come to mind as examples. On the individual level one recalls the heroics of Joan of Arc at Orleans in 1429. Of more interest to religion and the Afro-American community is the case of Nat Turner's explosion into history in 1831.

Like Joan, Turner was profoundly religious and thought himself in audio contact with Heaven. Also like Joan, the voices he heard spoke not to eschatology but to the immediate and mundane. Both figures presumed that death and the hereafter would take care of themselves if one listened to the quiet inner voice and made whatever on-the-spot improvements one could, whenever one could.

Joan petitioned the dauphin, who later became King Charles VII, for troops with which she defeated the British encampments at Orleans, on the Loire, and at Patay. Nat Turner surreptitiously recruited a ragtag little band of renegades and mounted the most successful slave insurrection in the history of the United States.

C and J could certainly be led to interpret their religion to mean that temporal self-help is as virtuous as the preparation for dying. And once an intellectual growth process is stimulated, no one can predict its limits. If one subscribes to the belief that enlightenment rises randomly in any community of humans, then one can believe that C and J would eventually begin toying with the idea of social improvement in ways unrelated to religion.

They would project social sympathies in the direction of their neighbors and out beyond their own communities as well, by this time relating to the world in three dimensions—seeing their own betterment in terms of the activities required to effect betterment, and in terms of the betterment of a wide area of humanity—all unrelated to religious admonitions.

In some philosophical circles this quality of morality is called humanism. But whatever the name, it was a morality applied to the pre-1865 southern social contract in small but perennial doses. It was sometimes applied by slaves, sometimes by indentured servants, and sometimes by free men; sometimes by blacks, sometimes by whites, and sometimes by integrated groups. The sum total of the moral applications had a profound effect on the outcome of American slavery.

8. Uprisings as a Result of Wide Concerns

As early as 1663, in Gloucester County, Virginia, unnamed groups of white indentured servants joined an equally unnamed group of slaves in a conspiracy to rebel. The local citizens celebrated the discovery of the plot with prayers of thanksgiving. Mr. John Smith's servant, who betrayed the plot, was granted his freedom.

In 1741 in New York City, twenty-five whites were arrested with 150 black slaves. They had set a series of destructive fires around town in protest of slavery. The seventeen ringleaders were burned alive in an integrated group. Others were hanged, and some were banished from the area.

Eight years before President Jefferson purchased the territory, three whites were charged with aiding and abetting a slave revolt in Pointe Coupee Parish, Louisiana. More than twenty slaves were executed, and the three whites were banished from the colony.

A series of trials followed the betrayal of Gabriel Prosser's conspiracy in Henrico County, Virginia, in 1800. The Prosser plot was the second largest organized by slaves in United States history. Intelligence was developed at the trials which implicated two white men as co-conspirators. Their names were never divulged, however, and they were never captured.

At another conspiracy trial two years later in the same county, a slave named Louis indicated that a number of poor white people had been involved in the plot. And another slave, Arthur Farrar, revealed that ten white men had promised to meet him at the magazine and give him guns and powder to carry out an uprising.

Two white men, Joe Wood and another named Macarty, along with a group of free Negroes, were implicated in a slave insurrection in New Orleans in 1812. Macarty was jailed, and Wood jailed and executed.

A white native of Virginia named George Boxley fretted about the plight of the slaves in and around Spotsylvania County for a number of years. He went off to serve in the War of 1812, and when he returned he decided to do something about the abomination. By 1816 he had organized a conspiracy which would free the slaves in Spotsylvania and some of the surrounding counties. When the plot was discovered and two dozen or more slaves were arrested, Boxley attempted to organize a rescue squadron. At that time he was arrested. But with implements smuggled to him by his wife, he escaped. One thousand dollars (at a time when prime farm land sold for one dollar per acre) was offered for his capture. George Boxley disappeared without a trace—except for an obscure footnote in the pages of history.

The largest slave conspiracy in American history was led by Denmark Vesey in Charleston, South Carolina, in 1822. Reliable estimates were that more than nine thousand people were involved. More than 130 Negroes and four white men were arrested when the plot was discovered. Thirty-four blacks were executed, and the four whites were fined and imprisoned.

Three hundred slaves and one white man were reported to have been involved in planning an ambitious insurrection in Macon, Georgia, in 1827.

A conspiracy in Hinds and Madison Counties, Mississippi, in 1835, involved fifteen slaves and six white men. They were all arrested and hanged. One of the whites, Ruel Blake, owned some of the slaves with whom he was hanged. Apparently he had become sufficiently revolted by the slavocracy to join the revolt against it.

Again in the same year, two other whites were hanged when a slave conspiracy was uncovered in East Feliciana, Louisiana.

A slave named Albert and a white schoolteacher named Dyson planned a conspiracy to free the Negroes of New Orleans in 1853. When the conspiracy was discovered and the two arrested, Albert testified that twenty-five hundred slaves were involved in the plot. Dyson indicated that more than a hundred whites had planned to aid the slaves in a variety of ways.

A white named William Mehrmann was discovered conspiring with two hundred slaves and a group of Mexicans in Colorado County, Texas, in 1856. Mehrmann and the Mexicans were chased out of the county. The slaves were arrested and whipped severely.

Three other such uprisings took place in different areas of the Confederacy during the same year. One included a few white men and a few hundred slaves in Union County, Arkansas. A second took place in the environs of Victoria, Texas. The occurrence was referred to as a large-scale insurrection. A number of whites were involved. One white was horsewhipped, and the others were driven from the county. The third insurrection was discovered in St. Mary Parish, Louisiana. In this one, a number of slaves, a free Negro, and three whites were arrested. The slaves were whipped, and one white and the free Negro were hanged.

9. John Brown

Then there was John Brown, often referred to in deference during his later years as the Old Man. He was Wood, Boxley, Blake, and Dyson all rolled into one—grown a little older, a little more experienced, and a bit more committed.

Brown had abhorred slavery all his life. As a young man in Ohio he aided fugitive slaves through the Underground Railroad to Canada. Through the years, the abolitionist fire burned away in his mind. His obsession with the evils of slavery kept him restless. Brown lived in a number of states over a wide area of the Northeast and Midwest, trying his hand at different jobs and various business ventures. Between the ages of forty-six and forty-nine he lived in Springfield, Massachusetts. There he operated a business for which he needed a warehouse. He used the structure more often as an Underground Railroad station than for its business purpose.

In his forty-ninth year, in an era when the average American male lived only forty to forty-five years, the Old Man organized a league of Negroes for the purpose of defending themselves against bounty hunters. And later that year Brown moved to North Elba, New York, a town which had been settled by Negroes.

In time Brown became weary of rallies, meetings, conventions, speeches, and monotonous invocations of moral suasion. The days of his life were winding down, and the end of slavery was nowhere in sight. The long panorama of horrors that had passed before his eyes over the years began to convince him that the despicable practice would never die as a natural result of civil and moral events. Slavery would have to be killed. Somewhere along the way he made up his mind to take drastic measures.

At the age of fifty-five Brown traveled westward again. This time he was ready to take a hand in the violence which had erupted along the Kansas-Missouri border.

A year earlier Congress had passed the Kansas-Nebraska Act, which repudiated the Missouri Compromise. The measure provided that questions concerning slavery in the new territories, even north of the 36° 30′ parallel, could be decided by the settlers. The doctrine was referred to as "squatters' sovereignty." Consequently, those who felt most strongly from both sides of the slavery issue rushed to settle the territory hoping to constitute the voting majority. And in the frontier atmosphere the long-festering disagreement boiled over.

It was into this physical and emotional cauldron of conflict that the Old Man arrived with a vengeance. During his sojourn there the territory became known as Bloody Kansas. Pro-slavery bands attacked and killed Free Staters in their villages, and the Free Staters reciprocated. For some time the contest seesawed back and forth, with the outcome hanging in doubt. For most of the duration of the contest, the pro-slavers seemed to have the upper hand. But the intrepid Free Staters hung on. They finally won the day when the territory adopted a constitution forbidding slavery. The Jayhawker victory confirmed Brown's conviction that violence was the only route by which slavery could be abolished.

Back east in Rochester, Brown visited and caucused with Fred Douglass. By this time Douglass was at the height of his power. He was the abolitionist movement's orator-in-chief, and its Exhibit One of what a slave, once freed, could become. For obvious reasons he was less than convinced, but thoroughly respectful, of Brown's advocacy of violence. And after the meeting Douglass distressed some of his moral suasion colleagues by sprinkling a few of Brown's sentiments in his speeches now and then.

The next time the two met, Douglass visited Brown. Already a fugitive from justice, the Old Man had summoned Douglass for a follow-up caucus at his hideout in an abandoned stone quarry near Chambersburg, Pennsylvania. Brown thought the time was ripe for a full-scale Jayhawker operation in the shadow of the nation's capital. He planned to seize the federal arsenal twenty miles to the south in Harper's Ferry. With the arsenal as headquarters, he would establish camps in the mountains at which runaway slaves could seek sanctuary, receive arms and supplies, and mount forays of their own to free additional slaves for Brown's "freedom army." Already he had the core of a war party around which the freedom army could be built. He wanted Douglass to join them.

Douglass was aghast. During their talk a few months earlier, he had agreed with Brown, in principle, that freedom was worth the spilling of blood, and that meetings, conventions, and rallies had their limits. But he was not prepared for the kind of immediacy Brown had in mind.

Douglass thought the attack on the arsenal was premature and ill-planned. As an assault on a federal installation it was also foolhardy. It would bring down the full weight of the United States armed forces on their heads. It would turn public opinion in both the North and the South against their cause, and would set back the carefully nurtured anti-slavery sentiment many decades.

Although each respected the other's opinion and judgment, neither of the opinionated contestants gave an inch of ground as the long night wore on. The caucus had started at 8:00 P.M. and continued full blast until 3:00 A.M. Orator and thinker that he was, Douglass at times found himself hard-pressed to hold his own against Brown. Brown stood for everything that Douglass stood for, and he advocated going about it directly and immediately, with a willingness to put his life on the line in the process.

Brown's eyes emitted a redeemer's gleam; a transcendent concentration and intensity which looked simultaneously at one and through one into the future beyond. He envisioned a future in which Douglass enjoyed the blessings of citizenship which he himself already had and held dear. And Brown was willing to make the down payment on the purchase price of his vision with his life. In another time and clime, when the literati were more spiritually than technically oriented, Brown would have been hailed a holy man.

At three o'clock, when they agreed to disagree, Douglass prepared to leave. He asked Shields Green, a hard-bitten fugitive slave who had accompanied him there, if he was ready to go. Green had listened stoically throughout the night as the argument alternately heated and cooled. And he indicated unhesitantly in a flat voice that he figured he would stay with the Old Man.

Douglass disappeared into the night and returned to the speaking circuit. A few days later, Brown moved onto the pages of history. He and his band of guerrillas, consisting of twelve white men, four former slaves, and one free Negro, captured the armory at Harper's Ferry.

The enterprise failed. Two days after the assault, Brown and those of his comrades who had not been killed in the raid were captured and turned over to the State of Virginia for trial. The state had its revenge, physically and propaganda-wise. Brown was hanged, and his captors were praised as brave men and true protectors of law and liberty. They were extolled as patriots and congratulated for having given fair warning to any other such treasonous renegades.

A number of Northern intellectuals and abolitionists heaped praise upon Brown, hailing him as a hero and martyr. Brown had a few last words of his own at his trial. He unrepentantly prophesied the Civil War; he thundered that his effort was a mild preview of things to come. But perhaps the most profound tribute to Brown's leadership and martyrdom came when Shields Green had spoken a second time. It had been during a lull of activity between the assault on the arsenal and their capture. A chance had arisen for some of the guerrillas to escape. One of the party had suggested to Shields that they seize the moment to fly away. Green's answer was that he thought he would just "stay and go down" with the Old Man.

Whatever opinions the citizens in and around Harper's Ferry (located then in the far north-central section of Virginia) had concerning the excitement in their town on October 16-18, 1859, they kept to themselves. But some idea concerning the substance of their sympathies might be inferred from their decision on June 20 of the fourth year following the arsenal drama. Harper's Ferry became the eastern-most town in the eastern-most county—uniquely surrounded on three sides by the Old Dominion—to attach itself to fifty-four counties farther west and become the State of West Virginia.

10. Wide-track Religion

The examples of indentured servants, bondsmen, and free individuals— some motivated by profound religious concerns and others by humanist considerations—all working for the redress of a grave social malignancy, indicated what can be accomplished. And except for the indentured servants and the bondsmen whose participation fell into the self-help category, the efforts demonstrated the wider, more noble concerns which had to do with the welfare of others. None of the ventures taken singly effected the change their protagonists sought, but taken together they generated the climate in which massive, change-producing engines perform. Relative to the Civil War, the accumulation of undertakings staged over the preceding two-hundred-year period created the gestalt in which the politicians, the war mobilization effort, and the Union Army functioned. And if religious and humanist endeavors could affect such an entrenched and long-sustained insti-tution as commercially profitable slavery, how much more quickly could such endeavors levitate C and J into the American mainstream of thought, aspiration, education, attitude, and conduct.

One-dimensional religious bondage is an ancestral malady of Afro-American society, an anachronism from which C and J have not recovered. One-dimensional religious bondage came in the package with physical bondage; imposed in lieu of a frontal lobotomy with the introduction to the English language. A conviction that one's temporal circumstances are of no consequence befits a bondsman's mentality. If one is convinced that his upcoming celestial reward will vary directly with his earthly tribulations, he is rendered further amenable to slavery—or to remaining an obedient tither. In either case, faith and the distrust of his own judgment are the stars he steers by, and humility is the course he charts.

No armies, logistics, or bloodlettings are necessary to release C and J from the debilitating fixations that ensnare them. The required undertakings are mental rather than physical. But heavy cognitive undertakings are incompatible with J's culture. It is for this reason that a careful hands-on effort is needed to direct his religious thrust into a new dimension.

Chapter 6
AFRO-AMERICAN LEADERSHIP AND FAITH

1. The Sources of Faith

It was not for nothing that the biblical patriarchs laid great store by faith. True, they articulated the idea narrowly in comparison with modern cosmopolitan concepts. But the centuries have eroded none of faith's authenticity. The patriarchs' worldview was that of the prehistoric tribesmen. They measured in days, for example, the distances no farther apart than today's metropolises and their jet ports.

Modern minds are exposed to the light of scientific knowledge as reflected in literature and the communications media. But, unfortunately, in overdoses light is as often bedazzling as it is revealing. In fact, discotheque devotees employ strobe lights specifically to induce vertigo.

In more simple and less confusing times, when far fewer "enlightenments" bombarded the mind, certain quiet inner lights shone through more clearly. The notion of faith may have been one of these insights—with validity for all time.

The ancients spoke of faith in terms of gods, behemoths, and eschatology—excursions among the stars and into the bowels of the earth. They spoke of a faith that cast out devils, cured the afflicted, and caused the beggar who lay crippled to roll up his pallet and walk.

The need for faith was self-evident in the straightforward relationship between the ancient herdsman and his son going about the daily care and defense of their flock. It was self-evident to the elder as he rested at night under the star-studded desert sky reviewing the day's work and planning for the next. Faith had a great deal to do with the way his son would carry on their tradition, and it factored into any hope there was for improvement. It still does. And now, as then, a fundamental faith powers the springboard from which civilizing traditions and lore are preserved and augmented. Every neophyte who moves on must have a mentor in whom he has faith; the tribesman's practical, workable, tested faith—uncomplicated, undiagnosed, unpsychoanalyzed, and uninstitutionalized.

Although faith has often been vitiated by priests, kings, institutions, and other repositories of power and opportunism, and its exploitive usage has necessarily bred cynicism, its essence remains incorruptible. Faith is at the basis of learning, and learning stops when cynicism sets in. In the same way, destructive precepts accrue when faith is misplaced.

Faith is based on love, respect, or a desire to please or emulate, singly or in some combination. The Afro-American male in the Jive community has never been in a position to inspire emulation in his son by the standards by which success is measured in the Atlantic Community. Once the male child grows beyond the infantile belief that his daddy can lick anyone else's daddy, his patriarchal respect degenerates to an unconscious contempt. Since he lives behind the one-way cultural filter screen, his contempt for his father often sifts through to the young males in the surrounding communities. This, in part, accounts for the fact that fewer Afro-American sons elect to follow in the career footsteps of their fathers than do sons of other ethnic groups.

The two prevailing attitudes absorbed by the Jive youth from his community ethos are defiance and resignation. The defiance manifests itself in a disdain for structure, order, and authority. The resulting frame of mind etches the hero's halo about the heads of the pimp, the illegal lottery operator, and all the assorted small-time hustlers freebooting in the streets. The adulation is constantly incremented as the outlaw, expending a modicum of effort and perspiration, fares increasingly better than the legitimate stoop wallah in his cul-de-sac.

In the short-range view of the short-range mind it is abundantly obvious that the mini-racketeer with his new gaudy clothes and expensive car is miles ahead of the straight little man—especially since "straight"and "legitimate" become increasingly associated with minimum-wage and catch-as-catch-can jobs.

The spokesmen who have Jive's ear do nothing to relieve his infirmity. They reinforce it. With the construction of a political power base of a "community development program" career in mind, they harangue away at the penalties and restrictions the "system" imposes on the youth. Never a word is expressed concerning the opportunities available in the system, or what the youth owes himself. Nothing is mentioned of plans that require more than a week's incubation time, nor are any downstream projections referenced. Only the resentment and defiance, and the youths' self-depreciation are nourished; appropriately packaged in a suggestive bravado.

Under an opportunistic leadership whip, and ensconced behind his one-way screen, Jive's racketeer worship assumes ominous refinements. To the degree that all his problems can be attributed solely to racism, and no self-help efforts can be realistically expected to succeed, various brands of humbuggery appear justifiable. And a great deal of thought goes into the development and justification of "angles." The point is regularly pursued so enthusiastically that even the outside youth receiving messages through the one-way screen is often caught up in the spirit of "achievement" through bluff, bombast, and blague.

Many middle-class parents are aghast when an offspring occasionally adheres to the lines of the apostles of defiance and despair taking their cues from the message emanating through the Jive enclave's one-way screen. Nor can they understand why their child, having grown up in their house listening to their philosophies, would choose to pursue the one-in-a-million gamble on a career in athletics or ephemeral pop music at the expense of their school work. Why, when the facilities and the accompanying parental sacrifice often required to go into the making of careers in engineering, science, law, or medicine are offered up on the altar of love and hope for the taking.

Should the spokesmen have the insight to coordinate their liturgy with the aspirations of the citizens in the community who have demonstrated the capacity to secure a foothold in the mainstream, the errant youth might transfer their faith to their parents, where quintessential faith belongs. The youngsters might give their parents' viewpoint a hearing rather than rejecting it simply because it is devoid of defiance and disillusionment. And the youngsters might believe, as they should, that their parents have their children's interests at heart; that within the twenty- or thirty-odd years beyond their own life-spans their parents just may have successfully encountered enough contingencies and vicissitudes to be able to render judgments of some value. In short, it might occur to the offspring that unlike the successive generations of less-developed primates—each of which has to learn through trial and error to fit the rods together to reach the high-hanging bananas in the often-conducted experiment—given the opportunity, human knowledge accumulates from generation to generation.

2. Confusing Love and License

Some parents are as confused as the college students who went into the rural South on behalf of voter registration in the 1960s became, or as the befuddled young school teachers of the seventies were. They try to rival the dress codes, hair styles, mannerisms, and inane repartee of the children to whom they are supposed to be giving guidance. A leadership worthy of the name would denounce this nonsense in short order. Instead, the foolishness is countenanced in the name of "relating to" the learner—another example of experimental education gone awry.

Still other parents manufacture endless excuses for their offspring who reject the values necessary for launching themselves into mainstream culture and technology. They develop the habit of condoning sloth instead of demanding excellence. Too many mothers and grandmothers indulge their young males. And indulgence is the most shortsighted and destructive form of love ever.

The Atlantic community media fallout over the past quarter-century verifies that in many ways the very rich and the insouciant poor have similar lifestyles. Theirs is signally less restrained than that of the middle sector of the population. The rich are able to act out many of humanity's wilder impulses and to indulge fantastic appetites because of their ability to pay their way out of any consequent troubles.

The unambitious poor can indulge their whims, fantasies, and appetites because they have nothing to lose in case of mishap. Having neither money nor property to forfeit, a stint in jail, usually with compatible fellows of easy restraint, often grants them a reprieve from the aggravations of life's gritty exigencies.

Civilization is kept afloat by the journeyman preoccupations of the middle classes. Significant deviations from their ideals result in failures to keep up in life's marathon. Afro-American spokesmen who espouse shortcuts and nonchalance ill-serve the youth whose ears they have.

3. J's Lack of Perspective

An obsession with racism implies a lack of historical perspective and a narrow contemporary view of reality. It ignores the considerable jockeying which always accompanies the contention for anything of value; the elbowing which takes place between competitors the world over, within and without the lines of race, nationality, ethnicity, and even family.

Down through the corridors of history into the present, more than a passing number of kings, chancellors, caliphs, generals, emperors, maharajas, and presidents-for-life have accorded their poor, ignorant, and helpless countrymen—of their own race and religion— fewer rights, opportunities, and civil liberties than Afro-Americans have possessed since the Civil War.

More incredible than C's and J's relationship to the storefront church is the symbolic rebellion against Christianity staged by another group—some of whom are supposedly educated and others, athletes of note. If one sifts out the ignorant, such a state of mind represents one of the monumental ironies of the time. They give lip service, based on scraps of the ideologies they only partly comprehend, and adopt the names prevalent in a region of the world where the grandees think so little of their own countrymen that illiteracy ranges between 50 and 88 percent, depending on the bailiwick. The average illiteracy for the area was 68 percent in 1977. If these armchair pioneers would tear themselves away from the gymnasium, playground, or television screen long enough to read so mundane a lexicon as the *World Almanac,* they might have cause for pause. In the heaven on which they have their eyes focused through the mists of misapprehension, they would be too poor, ignorant, and perhaps brutalized to realize they deserved anything so exotic as civil rights. Moreover, ecstasy there would consist of a good meal and a pair of hand-me-down sandals.

The voice that has Jive's ear might advise him that each Afro-American who reaches prominence makes it easier for the next who qualifies. The first introduces the country to an Afro-American presence in a new position and establishes a cultural and emotional acceptance. The phenomenon has already occurred in athletics and the performing arts, and is well along in other areas of American life.

4. J's Anti-preparation Philosophy

One consideration that the Jive community spokesman should have addressed long ago is the preparation for opportunity—on the horizon and beyond. An unfortunate resignation to the cultural maxim that honing one's equipment to cope with an opportunity yet unseen is a waste of time and a frustration is endemic to the community. This belief is in large part responsible for Jive's ongoing jealousy of the accomplishments of those with whom he identifies, except in sports and entertainment.

If one subscribes to the notion that preparation has no bearing on success, it follows then that success is the result of luck, dishonesty, compromising one's integrity, or selling out one's honor, ethnicity, or whatever else there is to be traded on. This gloomy creed is a logical extension of the resignation philosophy. Obviously the success-ful Afro-American has to be a thief, a tom, or a turncoat. And like dozens of other nonsensical ideologies, this one too often sifts through the one-way screen to pollute the areas around the Jive enclave.

The success-through-sports preoccupation, however, has Jive authenticity. It is an outgrowth of the Jive spokesman's philosophy of solving age-old problems with a single, flamboyant stroke. The line of thinking is also a linear descendant of his religious teacher's assurance that through mere faith one can, in time, enter through "pearly gates" to spend an eternity singing, feasting, shouting, and walking on golden streets, all without having to toil, sweat, or worry about the future. The belief in a sudden transition from misery to rapture has always had its hierophants who profiteered off the resigned.

One begins to wonder if the present spokesmen are capable of thinking outside the traditional protest groove, or whether those with the force and charisma to communicate with the excitable Jive mind recognize in the want ads of the metropolitan dailies the relationship between reality and their demands. If so, they would ascertain that the youth for whom they pretend to speak need training, skills, and education first and foremost. All the bellicosity in the world will not substitute for a certificate in electricity, plumbing, or automobile mechanics. All the complaining on earth about the unfair "system" will not open the way to the decent life that a degree in science or engineering would go far to ensure. And all the loitering about, "rapping," and awaiting a "break" will not do a fraction as well toward lifting one out of poverty and disarray as a functional knowledge of basic reading, writing, and reckoning.

Many examples of what the Jive youth should avoid could be drawn from the lives of their middle-aged and older neighbors, most of whom are unemployed—all in cul-de-sacs constructed of prolonged indiscipline. A small number, into whose heads life's knocks have cuffed insights rather than incoherence, aver that, if young again, they would conduct their lives differently, that a second chance at youth would be turned to good account. Their observations have no takers, however. By the age of twelve, Jive's cynicism and absence of faith have rendered his input antenna impervious to any idea not already in his mini-memory bank of experience. The introspective observations of his older neighbors strike him as the usual Jive babble. If the spokesmen who have his ear bothered to reinforce the opinions of the thoughtful among his elders, J might eventually begin to stir out of the haze which imprisons him.

Not all the young people who thrash about in self-destructive chaos and confusion can be turned around. But a clear-headed leadership could affect a sufficiently large number of them so that the black ghetto would not loom up immediately in the popular mind at the mention of poverty, illiteracy, family disorganization, and crime.

5. Lack of Faith in Political Spokesmen

Two of the ingredients of faith are its vocal affirmation and the conduct which demonstrates it. When the conduct belies the declaration, skepticism sets in in the community. Skepticism may be overt or unconscious, however. After all, who can question even the imperfect pursuit of high purpose? On the other hand, who can maintain real faith in a spokesman who advocates training, recreation, and pride, but stakes his reputation on an ability to acquire grant after grant for community surveys, studies, and plans—then perhaps for some shiny new playground equipment, on the off-chance that some financial residue might slosh over the rim of the travel-banquet-administrative receptacle? A spokesman who has faith in his constituency and who is worthy of its faith hews by work and deed, first and foremost, to the line of self-help—the best demonstration of faith. He realizes the pointlessness of supplying a deprived individual with venison jerky when he should be taught to fashion a bow and arrow. The need for provisions will arise day after day after day. With the bow and arrow and the skill to use it, one can provide for himself as the need arises. The deprived individual has no need to be studied and surveyed. The metaphysics of poverty and illiteracy are best left to social theorists and analysts whose objectives have to do with observation rather than alteration. The spokesman on the scene needs to confine his teaching to the construction and use of the tools for survival.

Many political spokesmen present their constituencies with problems of greater complexity than those posed by non-political spokesmen. In the process of jousting for position, advantage, and power, they forget their purpose. School boards in jurisdictions where C and J constitute numerical majorities furnish prime examples. Some members posture and caper for the sole purpose of drawing attention to themselves, hoping to draw enough klieg light exposure to justify running for bigger and better elective rewards, or at least to get another ride on the same carousel. Too often the ruse meets with success. It succeeds because the community's attention is diverted from its real problems. Emphasis is never put where it belongs. Outside agents are always blamed for the poverty of spirit and material in the enclave.

In league with the chastened, confused, and apologetic educators, the politicians seem to conspire to keep the students unenlightened. At the same time they would have the youth believe their interests are being served. The airwaves vibrate with declamations of sympathy for *our* children—who graduate illiterate and disadvantaged from high school, year after year. Any teacher, principal, or superintendent who betrays an inclination toward a strategy that ensures learning is in trouble, is pounced upon forthwith and unmercifully for being "elitist."

Both C and J love such politicians. They are the apples of the enclave's eye. They can be relied on to assault all the enemies that the enclave spokesmen have taught it to disdain. They are cool when it comes to enforcing regulations and hot when it comes to defending the miscreants' right to error and forgiveness. They are nonchalant in their own public conduct and that of their cronies but infuriated when their improprieties are pointed out. The politicians are *dégagé* about accounting for the funds for which they are responsible but torrid in pursuit of loans and grants in the name of their constituency— funds which, of course, they will "consent" to administer.

All in all, Jive's political spokesmen show as much contempt and as little respect for him as his non-political spokesmen. The entire spectrum of their words and actions indicate their conviction of Jive's helplessness and of his need for someone to ask alms in his behalf. At no time in the future do they expect Jive to become self-reliant. Even if given the instructions for success, which the spokesmen obviously think they have provided, Jive would be too dense to understand. Their entire thrust is toward keeping Jive fat, discontent, and manipulable. They have no faith in him.

6. A Need for Spokesmen Who Speak *to* Their Constituencies

Looking down the vistas of time, Washington envisioned the Afro-American assuming the status of a well-regarded citizen. Not only would he be grading roadbeds and driving steel, but he would be surveying rights-of-way and drawing up blueprints for railroads; not only stoking the boilers of railroad engines, but helping design and build them—all in proportion to his ratio in the population. But for the first step and the near future, Washington wanted to see the freedman building his own house, managing his acreage in a viable and productive way, plying his trade in the townships, and sending his children to school. He felt that as the Afro-American became a productive, property-owning, enlightened citizen in his community and cast off his role as a ward or a simple tool for exploitation, he would become an integral part of the community with all the rights, privileges, and responsibilities appertaining thereto.

Washington's antagonists saw citizenship as Botticelli saw Venus—rising full-grown from the sea—in this case, a sea of confusion, cross-purposes, and lacking in any depth of preparation. And unfortunately, in the way that base currency drives substantial currency from the marketplace, the quick-fix philosophy vanquished the more substantial idea from the popular mind. Thus the post-1965 spokesmen, as spiritual descendants of Washington's detractors, speak *for* and *on behalf of* their constituency, but not *to* it.

The arguments used by their spokesmen on their behalf are obviously alien and obscure to the rudderless youth in the Jive community. They have not the slightest grasp of unemployment percentages, gross national product projections, and mean, median, and average incomes, gaps, overlaps, and slippages. They hear from the television that they want jobs, but the jobs that fall into their purview are unattractive and non-rewarding. In their view, the time spent bottle-washing or bus-boying could be better devoted to hustling in the street. The rewards are more attractive and the activity more exciting.

So the very element for whom the spokesman pleads is the least sympathetic with what he advocates. Uninterested in what is requested in their name, the youth consider the exhortation just another example of Jive. They are often able to smile and crack wry jokes about the way the "fast-talking brother" is putting the "man" on. The "fast talk" would be more productively employed in an auditorium in the grammar school urging study and preparation for the future.

The majority of the youngsters about whose employment the spokesman hold forth have no idea of what goes into the capacity for holding a decent job. They see their spokesman on television, with a hair trim, usually, and dressed in a three-piece suit. But they have no concept of the effort that went into the spokesman's theological, business administration, or legal education. They see mechanics and attendants hopping in and out of pits at automobile races. But they know nothing of the expertise in ignition, timing, and power trains, or about the gears, transmissions, and differentials whose intricacies the nimble-footed attendants mastered before they were allowed to don the white coveralls or come near the high-performance machines. The youngsters see people sitting in fancy offices or going to even fancier restaurants. But they have no concept of the time, energy, exacting discipline, or determination that went into the degrees in engineering, economics, electronics, accounting, and journalism—or whatever it took to land a job in such an office, or to be able to afford to go to such a restaurant.

Exceptional individuals of all classes and times have perceived for themselves the subtleties that vibrate around achievers. No one had to tell Frederick Douglass that a difference existed between him and the planter who acquired, owned, and operated the domain on which he and his fellow bondsmen were enslaved. Not only was the baron different from the bondsmen, he was different from his overseer and the other poor whites who eked out a living on the fringes of the great man's holdings.

No one had to draw diagrams for Booker Washington to convince him that the circuit-riding school teacher, or the owner of the mine in which he worked, or even Mrs. Ruffner, his exacting employer who instructed him in the fine points of housework, were different from himself.

Both Douglass and Washington perceived in the haze-shrouded years of their early youth that a significant difference between themselves and the achievers they encountered was their own inability to read; to commune with the best, brightest, and most ennobling ideas of human civilization. Once this discovery was made and followed up by their resolve to rectify it, other revelations ensued in rapid succession. For example, they realized that achievers knew how to write, to reckon, and to think and express ideas clearly. They recognized edifying propositions and knew how to act on them.

Once the reader's curiosity is ignited, and provided his achievement burner is turned up, the qualities he needs to become the person he wants to be, and the methods of acquiring the qualities, become apparent.

Unaided perceptions and instinctive reactions are the qualities of the gifted, however. Ordinary individuals have to be repeatedly shown, exhorted, and drilled in the habits and states of mind that precede achievement.

Washington clearly understood the value of exhortation and drill. The post-1960 Afro-American spokesmen either fail to comprehend its importance, or choose to ignore it or leave it to someone else. And confusion and disarray reign where a functional edifice of progress should be erected.

The only achievements with which Jive identifies are circumscribed by athletics and entertainment, probably because athletics is so much more kinesthetic than cognitive, or because it is so thoroughly appealing to the excitable side of one's nature. From earliest childhood one understands the effort that goes into running, jumping, and twirling. Unsupervised children soon learn the techniques of both casual and violent body contact. Jive grows into manhood believing that life's highest calling consists of prevailing over other contestants in the physical arena; that the prizes and recognition for doing so constitute life's greatest triumphs.

It is quite possible that the modern Afro-American athlete has done too well for the good of the Jive community. His success and swaggering irreverence for the qualities that make for achievement in ordinary mortals distract the Jive youth from the pursuits upon which he should be focused—study, planning, and setting long-range goals, which represent achievements attainable through perseverance rather than special gifts. He is not a very useful model for Jive youth.

7. The "Roots" Game

The gravest sin perpetrated by the post-1960s spokesman on those who look to him for direction is his negligence in telling them what they need to hear in order to navigate in the Atlantic community. His second greatest transgression is the dilemma he poses to those who try to develop their own navigational skills. The spokesman advocates conflicting objectives. This practice has a historical, though thoughtless, precedent. It has been in unexamined use for so long that its lack of logic fails to register. It holds sacrosanct the duty of the Afro-American to maneuver himself into a position before the cornucopia and, simultaneously, warns him against dropping the attitudes and totems which keep him immobilized.

Succeeding in the modern world requires oscillating in resonance with it. Running the race in the electronic age cannot be done with one foot chained to the Jive gatepost.

Too many spokesmen tout racial pride as a contradiction to success. Their constituencies would be better served if the two were treated as separate entities. When mixed ineptly, the two spawn a grotesque array of conflicts. In one case, the Afro-American student, circa 1965, attended class in a famous eastern university carrying a rifle—to protect himself, he said. In another, there is the affluent middle-class Afro-American who has never tasted chitterlings, standing center stage at a racially mixed party, holding forth as a chitlin' chef. He has to "authenticate his roots." In still another case, one encounters the community-planning type, attending a meeting in full Brooks Brothers regalia, topped off with the ugliest dreadlocks imaginable. In an effort to demonstrate how adroitly he can walk both sides of the street, he succeeds in affirming his cultural schizophrenia.

Harkening back to one's roots is certainly a romantic idea. There are times and places where tipping one's hat to one's remote origins is proper and fitting. But a marathon is never won, nor even finished, by either the physically or culturally handicapped. No one should feel the need to say "we is" or the equivalent, in honor of a great-grandparent who never had the opportunity to go to school. Nor should one pretend to like chitterlings in consideration of a grandparent to whom no other protein was available. There are more appropriate Shinto rites. Providing one's progeny with increasingly greater opportunity is one of them. And if one's forebears could look back through the mists of time, "happiness" would be the sight of their distant offspring striding forward unencumbered by the cultural, physical, and historical handicaps under which they themselves struggled.

Many people lack the training and temperament to cope adequately with twentieth-century urban exigencies. They nurse a nostalgia for what they believe life was like at an earlier time. Many

Afro-American spokesmen play the "roots" game with these individuals. They postulate that life can be made bearable by returning to attitudes befitting Arcadian surroundings. These curbstone sages apparently forget—if they ever knew, limited readers that they are—that the "good ole days" had their horrors too, many more difficult to cope with than today's problems. Consider infectious diseases, for example. Typhoid fever, tuberculosis, pneumonia, and a host of other maladies—many whose names have gone out of popular use—ran rampant. People regularly died of blood poisoning, ear infections, and venereal "retributions" before the advent of "miracle" drugs. Countless thousands of people perished for the lack of a telephone to summon a physician—sometimes asleep no farther away than across town. Consider distance and travel. A relative who lived a mere hundred miles' distance away was practically lost from the family circle. And an arriving telegram usually announced the imminent or recent death of a loved one.

8. Reality Unrecognized

No doubt scores of sincere Afro-American spokesmen have aspired to leadership since the 1960s. They may even outnumber the humbugs two to one. Many have been caught up in the cultural slipstream that evolved in that decade. Protesting and demanding, both peacefully and disruptively, had been surprisingly rewarding. The resulting victories had been such peak experiences that the significance of the foothills of preparation below the rainbows of success have been lost.

A century of work had been invested in Afro-American education from the time the Christian missionary teachers followed the Union Army south until the early 1960s when their spiritual descendants taught in segregated schools ranging from one-room lean-tos to elite, urban learning sanctuaries. This was forgotten, if it had ever been internalized, by the television-nurtured extroverts upon whose shoulders the spokesman's mantle had fallen. They also ignored or discounted the long years and innumerable man-hours devoted to the legal training, research, preparation, and litigation that went into the terrain below the rainbows.

Advanced stages of the mentality that concentrates upon finding something to protest about provide a distorted concept of events at all levels of existence. And Jive's spokesmen reinforce his captious mentality and the attitudes and thought patterns that keep him an alien in his own country. The entire Jive community abounds with the conviction that hope is an illusion and that goodwill and good intentions are nonexistent. Where else, for example, would showing up at home with a bouquet of flowers at dinnertime be considered an unsolicited confession of recent perfidity? If "as a man thinketh, so he is" has any validity, no hope portends for an affinity group starting behind in the race for education, wage, and political parity that considers itself one-third lost rather than two-thirds abreast of the front rank.

In a permissive climate, the infectious negativism toward learning, work, progress, and the whole range of social relations and intercourse emanates with telling effectiveness through Jive's one-way filter screen. The results are more devastating in a "Me-ist" atmosphere than in one paying lip service, at least, to tradition, gentility, and the common good—especially to those who identify with the indigenous of the Jive enclave.

As late as the 1950s and early 1960s, Jive slapped his hand over his mouth and looked sheepish if an expletive chanced to escape his lips in public. He knew that those around him disapproved of such behavior. But that was before the "freedom school" fund-raisers dashed North in the denim haberdashery by which they identified with the field hands and popularized wearing jeans. Now Jive expands his chest and looks about defiantly in celebration of his expletives. Most of those around him approve of his lack of inhibition if not his ribaldry. And except for a few of the untrendy, the others tolerate his behavior without complaint. So, in a perverse way, J has become a social arbiter in the area of receation. Unfortunately, the community has not reciprocated by bestowing its work and study habits on Jive.

Expecting a series of handouts is antithetical to the state of mind through which self-reliance and self betterment are built. Biology, history, and conventional wisdom suggest that items which arrive as gifts cannot be maintained. Only the ability to acquire implies the ability to defend.

Maintaining that one's problems are solely the result of a malevolent "system" is keeping a hot air balloon of error afloat on the current of a defeatist dogma. Down through the ages one corner of Afro-American intellectualism has maintained that "a dream deferred dries up like a raisin in the sun." This is not true for those of Booker Washington's persuasion. Such a frame of mind has no intention of permitting its dream to dessicate. The dream may change as one moves through life's experiences, but it will not dry up as long as one is on his feet and able to keep it moistened with purposeful perspiration.

Those of the middle class who master the art of self-levitation and have cooperating progeny move into the elite business, professional, and intellectual circles and, eventually, into the pool of talent from which the Atlantic community leadership is drawn. Those with less artistry, drive, and luck remain in less important positions to supply the consistency and perspiration which cement the foundation of society, while they wait in hope for another turn of the generation wheel.

The middle-class state emits tense vibrations that elicit amused approval from the upper classes and perplexity and disdain from C and J.

9. Middle-class versus Jive Reality

Jive reality consists of mores and instincts that keep the community out of sync with mainstream rhythms. More than any other group, it needs exogenous leadership. The cap of its culture is cross-threaded, and too often its spokesmen are homegrown, with exaggerated views and responses to events.

When a mentor lets his neophytes off the disciplinary hook before they develop their own self-discipline, the novices' first reaction is to rejoice in their good fortune. Having gotten away without paying discipline's price, they think they have gotten a bargain or a "break." But in the inner core of their humanity they feel cheated, and the subliminal seeds of a wide variety of antisocial resentments begin to germinate.

For example, the Jive community is awash with a manifest disdain for the countless self-evident rules of community courtesy. Car horns blast throughout the hours of darkness over the enclave and its environs. It is especially bad around midnight, when the citizens who work are preparing to face the next day, and it is just as bad immediately after dawn, when the same workers would appreciate another half-hour of precious sleep.

Illegal parking is another hallmark of the Jive enclave and its surroundings. During the evening rush hours, dozens of cars stand blocking traffic on four-lane streets where the two curb lanes are used for neighborhood parking. The culprits would be easy to forgive except, in many instances, empty spaces are available two or three car-lengths away from where they sit defiantly with their blinkers flashing. The practice is so widespread that police patrol cars, on the rare occasions when they happen along, sit patiently awaiting their turn to pull around the double-parkers in order to proceed. Maybe the policemen have decided to ignore parking violations and concentrate their energies on more pressing infractions of the law. Or maybe they have simply given up in face of the magnitude of the task, realizing that an attempt to rectify minor violations and inconveniences would bring the community spokesmen down on their heads. There is the further possibility that the officers have been community fixtures for so long that they see nothing amiss with double-parking; no reason why the en-route traffic should expect the civility of uninhibited passage through the streets.

The double-parking syndrome is only the tip of the iceberg of contempt for order and propriety. Broken bottles, beer cans, paper plates, cups, and chicken bones are strewn from cars cruising through the neighborhood in which the drivers live.

Pandering to the ignoble complaints and excuses for drift instead of pressing for a code of acceptable conduct and accountability is the ultimate manifestation of the spokesman's lack of faith in the youth. A vague consciousness of this mentality constitutes the core of J's reciprocal lack of faith in his spokesmen. Apologizing for shabbiness and sloth is no way to gain the respect of the confused. Votes may be garnered in the precincts in many instances, and shouts of "right on" may rend the air in response to a nonsensical speech, but these are not the ingredients that go into the making of faith and respect.

It is because of the absence of leadership that faith, for all practical progressive purposes, is nonexistent in the Jive enclave. Faith cannot germinate and survive in so sterile an environment. Faith in oneself, for example, as opposed to bluff and bluster, begins as one works at what appears to be a difficult project and sees accomplishment materialize. An introduction to faith-building circumstances requires a mentor for all but the most exceptional of individuals.

If one is never steered, inspired, or forced into a difficult project and encouraged to persevere, one never becomes acquainted with the bricks and mortar with which one builds one's faith in oneself. And faith in oneself, a spiritual cut above self-confidence, is the beginning of an understanding of the need and requirements for self-improvement.

The desire to improve oneself and one's surroundings is the essence of humanness. The characteristic is naturally as strong in the Jive enclave as it is elsewhere. However, it is thwarted and misguided there. The quality is evident in the grotesque dress and conduct of the inhabitants and in their mode of conspicuous consumption, often practiced at the expense of essentials, and all designed to draw favorable attention to the individual's identity and worth.

The conflict between a human desire to escape humdrum and disorder and the cultural attraction toward mental and physical squalor sparks a destructive tension—a tension which leaves room for nothing except discontented drift and a dull hope for excitement, any form of excitement: a fight, a fire, or even a riot or a looting spree.

The antisocial manners and behavior resulting from the desire for a better life without understanding its prerequisites, or even that it has prerequisites, represent some of the many facets of the ethics of deprivation. Deprivation metaphysics permits the maiming or murder of a comrade over the "principle" involved in a dispute about a quarter. It allows assault on senior citizens in one's own neighborhood in order to get the few pennies they have left after the purchase of medicine from the local apothecary, or merely for "fun." It sanctions the willful destruction of property for no better reason than the "excitement" of hearing the crashing, crunching, splintering sound of metal, wood, or glass. And it denies anyone caught up in its throes the embarrassment usually associated with grotesque modes of dress and speech. A sincere and knowledgeable spokesman offering up a proper oar could make inroads into the entire array of disabilities simultaneously. If a fraction of the energy devoted to deriding the evils of the "system" were spent implementing training programs, great chunks could be clawed out of the conduct and unemployment scrap pile.

10. Introspective Leadership Needed

Whenever J's spokesmen take to the stump, they pronounce their client's condition worse than when last reported. One wonders whether they examine their own roles in his destiny. If his condition has been deteriorating since the 1960s, he has been listening to the wrong speeches and following the wrong pied pipers.

Their melancholy texts should be rewritten. The counsel of despair should be deleted, and the villain theory of society revised. A paragraph of instructions concerning the disadvantages of self-destructive practices, habits, and attitudes should be inserted. A few lines should be added pointing out the advantages of self-control and planning and order. And a complete new positive philosophy, with instructions to justify it, should replace the victim mentality.

Debates should be organized: It should be recognized that the cardinal Jive disabilities are generated within the enclave rather than imposed from without. Such a discussion would ferment enough useful introspection to turn hundreds of lives around. If one insists upon calling himself a "man," as J ritually does, his spokesmen should give him some historical reminders of manhood's essence. A man improves his condition against whatever odds he encounters. When not faring well, he determines whether his condition is the result of his environment or his own ineptitude in interfacing with it.

Since the origin of species, survivors have taken one of two courses vis-à-vis harsh habitats: either adjustment or migration. And migration does not always imply crossing oceans, continents, or even mountains. Sometimes it entails a migration of the mind. From its beginning, civilization has been an ever-accelerating process of subordinating the physical to the conceptual. And those groups left too far behind in the disciplined intellectual race have suffered the consequence of ineptitude.

J deserves leaders willing to recast rather than reinforce his infrastructure. A clinical rather than an emotional assessment of the problems is needed. The task requires faith that a badly addressed group can, with proper tutelage, turn losing habits and attitudes into winning ones. The task can be accomplished. And it *will* be when J's current spokesmen assume a wide-track stance and become leaders like some of their illustrious predecessors.

SELECTED BIBLIOGRAPHY

Aptheker, Herbert. *Negro Slave Revolts in the United States 1526-1860.* New York: International Publishers, 1939.

———. *The Negro in the American Revolution.* New York: International Publishers, 1940.

Bennett, Lerone, Jr. *The Negro Mood.* New York: Ballantine Books, 1964.

Dann, Martin E. *The Black Press 1827-1890.* New York: G. P. Putnam's Sons, 1971.

Foner, Philip S. *Frederick Douglass.* New York: International Publishers, 1945.

Frazier, E. Franklin. *Black Bourgeoisie.* New York: Free Press, 1962.

Hogben, Lancelot. *Mathematics for the Million.* New York: W. W. Norton, 1943.

Lawson, Elizabeth. *Thaddeus Stevens.* New York: Elizabeth Lawson, 1962.

Lincoln, C. Eric. *The Negro Pilgrimage in America.* New York: Bantam Books, 1967.

Lomax, Louis E. *The Negro Revolt.* New York: Ballantine Books, 1964.

Mathews, Basil. *Booker T. Washington, Educator and Interracial Interpreter.* College Park, Md.: McGrath Publishing Co., 1969.

Ortega y Gasset, José. *The Revolt of the Masses.* New York: W. W. Norton, 1932.

Penn, I. Garland. *The Afro-American Press and Its Editors.* New York: Arno Press, 1969.

Russell, Bertrand. *Wisdom of the West.* London: Rathbone Books, Ltd., 1959.

Wells, H. G. *The Outline of History.* New York: Doubleday, 1949.

Wolseley, Roland E. *The Black Press, U.S.A.* Ames, Iowa: Iowa University Press, 1971.